OSCAR WILDE was born in Ireland in 1854, and died in Paris 46 years later, after a life filled with fame and scandal. He had already begun to make a literary reputation as an undergraduate at Trinity College, Dublin, and Magdalen College, Oxford, where he received the Newdigate Prize for Poetry. When he was twenty-seven a collection of poems appeared, and was followed by THE HAPPY PRINCE AND OTHER TALES (1888). Ten years later, his famous novel, THE PICTURE OF DORIAN GRAY, appeared. Then, in rapid succession, the plays. Wilde is credited today with the revival of the theater tradition of Congreve and Sheridan. He called THE IMPORTANCE OF BEING EARNEST "A Trivial Comedy for Serious People," noting that its first act is "ingenious," the second "beautiful," and the third "abominably clever." The play satirizes birth, love, marriage, death and respectability — everything that man considers important.

HENRY POPKIN serves as drama critic of *Vogue*, reviews New York theater for the London *Times*, and has contributed to the New York *Herald Tribune*, *The New York Times*, *Kenyon Review*, *Sewanee Review*, *Commentary*, *Tulane Drama Review*, *New Republic*, *New Leader* and other periodicals. He has recently edited *New British Drama*, a revised edition of Barrett H. Clark's *European Theories of the Drama*, and *The Concise Encyclopedia of Modern Drama*

Oscar Wilde

The Importance of Being Earnest

AN AUTHORITATIVE TEXT EDITION

Critical Material Selected and
Introduced by Henry Popkin

AVON BOOKS
An Imprint of HarperCollins*Publishers*

AVON BOOKS
An Imprint of HarperCollins*Publishers*
195 Broadway
New York, NY 10007

Introduction and text copyright © 1965 by Avon Book Division, The Hearst Corporation
Cover illustration by Alex Tsao
ISBN: 0-380-01277-4
www.avonbooks.com

First Avon Books printing: January 1965

Avon Trademark Reg. U.S. Pat. Off. and in Other Countries, Marca Registrada, Hecho en U.S.A.
HarperCollins® is a trademark of HarperCollins Publishers Inc.

Printed in the U.S.A.

80 79 78 77 76 75

ACKNOWLEDGMENTS

Material from *The Letters of Oscar Wilde*, edited by Rupert Hart-Davis. Copyright © 1962 by Vyvyan Holland. Used by permission of Rupert Hart-Davis Ltd.

Excerpts from *The Importance of Being Earnest: A Trivial Comedy for Serious People in Four Acts as Originally Written*, edited by Vyvyan Holland. Copyright © 1956 by Torquil John Murdoch MacLeod, Trustee. Published by the New York Public Library and reprinted by permission of Vyvyan Holland.

"An Old New Play" from *Our Theatres in the Nineties* by George Bernard Shaw (1932). Reprinted by permission of The Public Trustee and The Society of Authors.

"The Importance of Being Earnest" from *Around Theatres*, by Max Beerbohm. Copyright © 1930 by Max Beerbohm. Reprinted by permission of Rupert Hart-Davis Ltd.

"Oscar Wilde and the Theatre" from *James Agate: An Anthology*, edited by Herbert Van Thal. Copyright © 1961 by Rupert Hart-Davis Ltd. Reprinted by permission of the publisher.

Contents

Contents

INTRODUCTION

Like Dr. Johnson, but without the aid of a Boswell, Oscar Wilde is an author whose personality endures more vividly than most of his writings. I hasten to add that *The Importance of Being Earnest* endures, and so do some of Wilde's essays and "The Ballad of Reading Gaol." But, like *Rasselas,* "The Vanity of Human Wishes," and Johnson's other permanently interesting writings, they comprise a rather modest residue for a lifetime of literary work.

If Wilde's personality has outlasted most of the words he put on paper, it is still a personality intimately connected with his writing. If we may believe his friends, he expressed himself best and most characteristically in his high-spirited, infinitely resourceful, ingenious conversation. When he first came to London, he was an ostentatious "character" who affected an outlandish costume, but his true reputation overcame this notoriety, only to be eclipsed in turn by the scandal that ended his career.

Among his many friends, Wilde enjoyed the greatest distinction as a wit, as an irrepressible dazzler on all occasions. Max Beerbohm told S. N. Behrman: "Well, in the beginning he was the most enchanting company, don't you know. His conversation was so simple and natural and flowing—not at all epigrammatic, which would have been unbearable. He saved that for his plays, thank heaven." Fortunately, Wilde knew enough to preserve his witticisms, and not only the epigrammatic ones. If his rapt listeners did not include a Boswell, he compensated for this deficiency by being his own Boswell, preserving his wit in his literary work. Connoisseurs among his acquaintances preferred his jokes and stories in the form he gave them as he spoke, but we who are Wilde's posterity are beggars who cannot be choosers. Accordingly, we read his novel, *The Portrait of Dorian Gray*, and such plays as *Lady Windermere's Fan* and *An Ideal Husband*, seeking the occasional plum, the bright remark couched in Wilde's distinctive style. But the witticisms work best in a setting that is worthy of them, and they got such a setting only in *The Importance of Being Earnest*. Only this work, Wilde's last completed play, is a feast of such plums, the only one of his plays that is consistently written in his highest and wittiest style, the conversational style that belonged peculiarly to Wilde himself.

Invariably, wit comments upon its opposites, slowness of thought and infelicity of expression; implicitly, it ridicules dullness and solemnity. In his previous plays, Wilde had softened his attack upon ordinary reality by creating some good, dull people who carried on the necessary business of the main plot. But *The Importance of Being Earnest*, being wholly dedicated to wit, presents good, dull people only to caricature them. The brightly burnished style of this play directly comments upon the drabness of ordinary speech, and, indeed, it defies the real world. Defiance was always part of Wilde's public attitude, but only in *The Importance of Being Earnest* was he so bold as to make this defiance plain from the beginning to the end of the play. Even his two plain speakers embody a highly stylized plainness, Philistinism cubed, as it were, and the one plainer speaker disappeared while the play was being cut for performance. As it stands, this comedy is the fullest embodiment of Wilde's lifelong assault upon commonplace life and commonplace values. It was inevitable that the conventional world should strike back at Wilde, at his character and his ideas, if not specifically at his play, but the speed and cruelty of the world's retribution surpassed expectation. Four days after the opening of his last and finest comedy, the succession of events began that brought about his disgrace, imprisonment, and exile.

Wilde's defiance, it should be understood, was deeply personal. It was not at all the product of any seriously considered social criticism, but, rather, it stemmed from an individualism supported by a philosophy of art for art's sake. I find it significant that George Woodcock, in the principal study of Wilde's social thought, discovers some trenchant, if incidental, social criticism in the earlier plays, but next to nothing of this element in *The Importance of Being Earnest;* accordingly, he dismisses Wilde's masterpiece with a single sentence. But this play is not only Wilde's masterpiece; it also has the virtue of expressing its author more fully than any of his other dramatic or narrative writings. Mr. Woodcock to the contrary notwithstanding, it does criticize society, but not from the usual standpoint of social reform. Wilde attacks society on aesthetic grounds, in this play as in his previous works. What he recommends to us, and by implication only, is not social reform, women's suffrage, or child-labor laws, but style —a style of life, of behavior, and of speech. By showing the height of wit and manners, he criticizes their absence. This may not sound much like anyone else's kind of social criticism, but it is Wilde's critique of society, and it fulfills the logic of his life as an artist up to that moment.

The beginning of his life was surely conducive to individualism, if not to art. He was the product of an eccentric Dublin family—Oscar Fingal O'Flahertie Wills Wilde, second son of a prominent physician, William Wilde, and Jane Elgee Wilde, who, as "Speranza," wrote articles and verses passionately urging liberty for Ireland. William Wilde was a notorious philanderer and the father of several illegitimate children; once his wife wrote a private letter chiding one of his former mistresses and was promptly sued by the lady in question in an action that anticipated Oscar Wilde's suit against the Marquis of Queensbury for libel by private correspondence. The dramatist was born October 16, 1854, but later, so that he might seem even more of a prodigy than he really was, he represented himself as having been born in 1856, a year that is still sometimes recorded as the date of his birth.

In school he was not at first a good student, but he improved at Trinity College, Dublin, where he studied classical literature under J. P. Mahaffy, with whom he subsequently traveled in Italy and Greece. He entered Oxford University in 1874; there he won academic honors for his work in the classics, began to be known as a "character," and came under the influence of John Ruskin and Walter Pater. Ruskin's reformist social philosophy was less attractive to him than the aestheticism of Pater, who wrote in his *Studies in the History of the Renaissance*: "To burn always with this hard, gem-like flame, to maintain this ecstasy, is success in life." Pater concluded with praise of "the desire of beauty, the love of art for its own sake. . . . For art comes to you, proposing frankly to give nothing but the highest quality to your moments as they pass." In conversation with Yeats, Wilde said of this volume: "It is my golden book; I never travel anywhere without it; it is the very flower of decadence; the last trumpet should have sounded the moment it was written." Even when we allow for Wilde's inclination toward hyperbole, it is clear that he was profoundly affected by Pater's teaching that art and beauty were the primary values in life. He espoused Pater's aestheticism with a vigor that evidently dismayed his old teacher; reviewing *The Portrait of Dorian Gray*, Pater warned against neglect of "the moral sense."

In London, Wilde came to know the famous of the literary and theatrical world, wrote romantic poetry, and adopted peculiar attire. He would wear knee breeches, a velvet jacket, and black silk stockings, and he would carry a sunflower or a lily in his hand. All this was part of his pose as a dandy, a living embodiment of studied frivolity in behavior and particularly in dress, heir to the dedicated dandyism of Beau Brummel and Disraeli. Dandyism did more than poetry to win Wilde his first fame. He was lampooned in *Punch* and in an opera by Gilbert and Sullivan, *Patience,* in which he became Bunthorne, the young man "anxious for to shine in the high aesthetic line" and consequently to be seen walking "down Piccadilly with a poppy or a lily in your hand." It was evidently in order to get some publicity for *Patience* that the impresario D'Oyly Carte arranged for Wilde to give a series of lectures in America. Wilde enjoyed an unbroken series of triumphs, from Boston to Leadville; at Camden, he met Whitman, who found him "genuine, honest and manly." Even in unlikely circumstances, his forthrightness and his wit won him friends; it was an experience that he was to repeat many times, even when he met his archenemy, the Marquis of Queensbury, for the first time.

Just before and after his trip, he wrote his first plays, two melodramatic and uncharacteristic works, *Vera: or The Nihilists* and (in verse) *The Duchess of Padua.* In the years that followed, he lectured, edited *The Woman's World,* wrote a play, *Salome,* in French (interpreting Salome as being inflamed by thwarted love for John the Baptist), and published stories, essays, and poems. Among his essays, "The Critic as Artist" is useful for its formation of Wilde's ideas. The first half of this dialogue asserts the independent dignity of criticism; the second half ranges farther, affirming "All art is immoral"——a statement which Wilde interprets as meaning that art has no connection with morality, not that art opposes morality——and pleading the superiority of art to life: "Don't let us go to life for our fulfillment of our experience.... It is through Art, and through Art only, that we can realize our perfection; through Art, and through Art only, that we can shield ourselves from the sordid perils of actual existence." The doctrines of "The Decay of Lying" betray the same preference for art over life, and here Wilde's playful approach leads him to a defense of falsehood that can help to explain the great amount of highly imaginative lying in *The Importance of Being Earnest*. He celebrates "the true liar, with his frank, fearless statements, his superb irresponsibility, his healthy, natural disdain of proof of any kind" and roguishly assails the United States, "that country having adopted for its national hero a man who, according to his own confession, was incapable of telling a lie."

Wilde's fiction and drama almost invariably tend to give prominence to some secret sin—and, indeed, *The Importance of Being Earnest* is no exception, for both of its heroes assume false identities to sow their wild oats. Sin, in these stories and plays, might well have been defined by their author as original behavior. The creative sinner acknowledges the world only by concealing his sin, not by regretting it. Without intending to do so, Wilde virtually states the rationale for his sinners in "The Critic as Artist":

> What is termed Sin is an essential element of progress. Without it the world would stagnate, or grow old, or become colorless. By its curiosity Sin increases the experience of the race. Through its intensified assertion of individualism, it saves us from monotony of type.

Accordingly, the hero of the story "Lord Arthur Savile's Crime" commits a necessary sin with no qualm of conscience and conceals it only because conventionality and the law compel him to. A character in "The Portrait of Mr. W. H." hypothesizes that Shakespeare's secret sin was a homosexual relationship with a boy actor. In *The Portrait of Dorian Gray*, Dorian follows to the letter the advice he gets from the author's spokesman, Lord Henry, and so devotes his life to the pursuit of selfish pleasure. He commits two murders, causes the suicide of a girl who loves him, and no doubt commits many more sins, making good use of his gift of eternal youth in concealing them. At last, he is incomprehensibly punished for his original behavior—incomprehensibly if we consider the context of the novel and of the rest of Wilde's work and thought. Take, for example, his abandonment of his fiancée. Her love for Dorian has the effect of making her a bad actress, and thus, by preferring life to art, she violates one of Wilde's most basic principles; with perfect logic, Dorian drops her.

The plays that precede *The Importance of Being Earnest* also have their full complement of secret sins. In *Lady Windermere's Fan* (1892), the secret sin is the illegitimate birth of Lady Windermere, who knows nothing of her origin and despises her unacknowledged mother, Mrs. Erlynne. The sin remains hidden, but Lady Windermere learns a little respect for the virtuous sinner, her mother. Mrs. Erlynne's trespass produces some palpable benefits, thus living up to Wilde's advertisement for sin in "The Critic as Artist." Mrs. Erlynne has brought an excessively virtuous young lady into the world and has later happened along just in time to save that virtuous lady's reputation. It would seem that, without sin, there could be no virtue; long ago, Chaucer's Wife of Bath said much the same.

Wilde repeats this pattern in the next two plays, making secret sin the necessary source of good. The secret sin of *A Woman of No Importance* is again an illegitimate birth. Once more, the illegitimate offspring is a most virtuous young person, and his virtue moves his negligent father to a belated and useless repentance. In *An Ideal Husband,* a politician has, long before, sold a state secret and thereby begun a genuinely useful career in public life; he is threatened by a blackmailer who is eventually rendered harmless. Over and over, then, the sin is beneficial or harmless or at least defensible on philosophical grounds (as in *The Portrait of Dorian Gray*), but concealment is always necessary, and retribution always threatens. It is easy enough to detect a connection with Wilde's own secret sin.

In 1884, Wilde married Constance Lloyd, a loyal, affectionate woman who shared little of his life in the great world. She bore him two sons, in 1885 and 1886. It was apparently in the latter year that his homosexual practices began, and then the parables of secret sin followed. In 1891, Wilde met a young beginner in poetry, Lord Alfred Douglas; in three years, their attachment had become so notorious that it was the subject of Robert Hichens' novel, *The Green Carnation,* which was first published anonymously and which Wilde gracefully disclaimed. Furious with Wilde and only temporarily mollified by a personal meeting with him, Douglas' father, the eccentric Marquis of Queensbury, tried to create a scene at the opening of *The Importance of Being Earnest* in 1895; he was barred from the theater, and so he contented himself with sending an abusive note to Wilde at his club. Wilde sued for libel, lost his case, and was himself tried for immoral practices and found guilty. He served two years in prison and emerged a broken man. He spent his last years in France, and, during his final exile, wrote his celebrated poem of prison life, "The Ballad of Reading Gaol." In prison, he had written his long letter to Douglas, "De Profundis," which has only recently been published in its entirety. Earlier editions included only Wilde's expression of the infinite tragedy of his own situation and omitted the accusations he leveled at Douglas. Wilde died in Paris in 1900 with a last epigram: "I am dying, as I have lived, beyond my means."

The Importance of Being Earnest is the only play in which Wilde freed himself from melodrama and from a tendency toward unfelt, unconvincing moralizing. In the plays just preceding, the so-called "society" plays, a suspenseful, melodramatic plot dominates, and the one witty character utters his aphorisms in a sort of vacuum. Each wit is a dandy, a lord, and, at least in intention, a villain. (Lord Goring, of *An Ideal Husband,* offers, to be sure, no more than the hopeful promise of the "bad qualities" to which he lays claim.) Add to the three dandy-lord-villain types of the "society" plays Lord Henry Wotton, the elegant theorist of evil in *The Portrait of Dorian Gray,* and we get a rather full impression of Wilde's mixed feelings about the dandy. The dandy is brilliant and admirable, but, at the same time, he may deserve the punishment which befalls the dandy of *A Woman of No Importance* and the dandy's protégé in *The Portrait of Dorian Gray*. No mixed feelings, and certainly no guilt feelings, enter the portrait of the dandies in *The Importance of Being Earnest*. Here we have two of them, of whom one, Jack, is the rather solemn nominal hero, and the other, Algernon, gets more of the witty lines. Both live double lives, and their presumable sins constitute the play's feeble echoes of the scarlet career of Lord Illingworth and Dorian Gray. Each chooses to sin in a special place—Jack in the city and Algernon in the country. What shameful deeds, what unforgivable sins do they commit when we find them, each in turn—Jack in the first act and Algernon in the rest of the play—in the special area allotted to his wickedness? Each is confronted by an estimable young lady, and each takes no baser advantage of the occasion than to propose marriage. Four days before the beginning of exposure and subsequent disaster, Wilde is sufficiently carefree about secret sin to be here lampooning the idea.

The pursuit of marriage in this play is one more instance of Wilde's favorite pattern: the pursuit of pleasure. The young men of the play pursue pleasure in their "Bunburying," in their proposals of marriage, and in their elegant attire and speech. They lie for the sake of the pleasure an ingenious lie can give, in accordance with the ideas Wilde expressed in "The Decay of Lying." In a characteristic moment, Algernon catches Jack in a lie and hopes for more: "Now produce your explanation, and pray make it improbable." In an uncharacteristic moment, Jack finds that he has been telling the truth and asks his fiancée if she can forgive him. Gwendolen rises to the occasion: "I can. For I feel that you are sure to change." Lying is second nature to the people of this play, and, in the matter of the missing cucumbers, Algernon's manservant lies with an effortless grace that must come of careful training and long practice. Falsehood has the complex advantage of mixing pleasure, creativity, convenience, and the defiance of conventional morality—an irresistible combination.

Another way to mock conventional morality is to fit a solemn tone to a frivolous content. That is part of the secret of the name Ernest; none of the young people of the play is truly earnest, but all, and especially Jack and Gwendolen, are earnest in manner. When *The Importance of Being Earnest* is properly performed —as it was in the production that Sir John Gielgud brought to America in 1947—it has a perfect, a majestic dignity. As Gielgud himself has said: "Everybody is solemn, correct, polite." Even in the scene in which Jack and Algernon stuff themselves with muffins, quarreling all the while: "The decorum, the deadly importance of the triviality, is everything—they are greedy, determined, but exasperatedly polite." To be so solemn over such trivial matters, over muffins or over a Christian name, is to make fun of solemnity itself, to lampoon the possibility that anything can be taken seriously. That is what Wilde had in mind when he interpreted the play to his friend Robert Ross. Ross asked: "What sort of play are we to expect?" The dramatist answered: "It is exquisitely trivial, a delicate bubble of fancy, and it has its philosophy." "Its philosophy?" "That we should treat all the trivial things of life seriously, and all the serious things of life with sincere and studied triviality."

A more direct assault upon solemnity is made when the people of the play speak their irreverent aphorisms as if they are the inherited, proverbial wisdom of the ages. The easiest way to imitate a proverb is actually to cite a proverb, making a few incidental changes that turn its meaning upside down. Accordingly, the characters say: "Divorces are made in Heaven. . . . It is simply washing one's clean linen in public. . . . I hear her hair has turned quite gold from grief." To invert these respectable, conventional clichés is to subvert respectability and conventionality themselves, and that is just what Wilde intended. He is saying that respectability is tiresome, repetitious, unoriginal; in short, he is applying an aesthetic judgment by bringing in the contrasting brightness and inventiveness of his witty characters. On one occasion, Wilde permits a more direct equation to be made between respectability and ugliness. Asked if Miss Prism is "a female of repellent aspect," her suitor, Canon Chasuble, indignantly, if irrelevantly, declares: "She is the most cultivated of ladies, and the very picture of respectability." Lady Bracknell knows the old drudge at once: "It is obviously the same person."

Since *The Importance of Being Earnest* is often assigned to the category of "high comedy," we may expect to find that it shares some traits with plays belonging to the great period of English high comedy, the Restoration. For purposes of this comparison, if not for a definitive analysis of Restoration comedy, I find it useful to employ the approach of T. J. Fujimura in *The Restoration Comedy of Wit*. Fujimura finds, at the heart of Restoration comedy, a competition in wit; the competitors fall into three principal classifications: Witwoud (the vain, self-deluding fop who tries too hard to be fashionable and witty), Truewit (the golden mean of wit, fashion, and common sense), and Witless (the rustic boor who knows nothing of fashion or wit and so does not strive to excel). It is easy enough to find Wilde's candidates for the last classification: the two country boors, Miss Prism and Canon Chasuble, whose wit is invariably unintended. Jack and Algernon are obviously dandyish masters of wit and fashion, but close attention to them will surely reveal that Wilde has blurred the distinction between Witwoud and Truewit; Algernon in particular, since he is the wittier of the two, does not know the meaning of excess. He defends himself with the vanity of a true fop: "If I am occasionally a little overdressed, I make up for it by being always immensely overeducated."

Algernon's delight in himself and his wit reminds us of the prominence of pleasure in all the action of the play. Wit is self-indulgence, and so is Bunburying, so is courtship, so is Lady Bracknell's concern for wealth and position, and so is the voracious eating that goes on continually. But these characters are soundly practical as well, as Algernon and Cecily remind us when, for the sake of a dowry, they agree to postpone marriage till Cecily is thirty-five. Practicality is Lady Bracknell's forte, and at the other extreme are Miss Prism and Canon Chasuble, who are too dull and too moralistic even to be practical. Obviously, in Wilde's scale of values, the moralizing of this pious couple ranks very low indeed, well below the values of pleasure and practicality.

What magic is in that name Ernest? Its peculiar value seems to be only that it gives pleasure to Gwendolen and Cecily. Their fondness for it is as irrational as most preferences, and so, characteristically, each associates it with different qualities, Gwendolen with steadiness, indeed, earnestness, and Cecily with frivolity. One of the Ernest-hunters must remain forever unsatisfied, but Wilde chooses to ignore this point and to leave Cecily content with her Algernon. The quest for Ernest and the quest for Jack's identity—they turn out to be the same in the end—both recall the melodramatic well-made play that would be constructed upon a guilty secret, in fact, just like *Lady Windermere's Fan* or *An Ideal Husband,* except that Wilde is here burlesquing the kind of play he used to write. Gerald Arbuthnot, of *A Woman of No Importance,* learns his true identity just as abruptly, just as coincidentally, as Jack Worthing, the only difference being that, in the later play, Wilde acknowledges the absurdity of the situation.

The Importance of Being Earnest was presented by the actor-manager George Alexander, who had staged and acted in *Lady Windermere's Fan;* Alexander, a romantic leading man, whose polished manner was well suited to the grave tone of the play's surface, played Jack Worthing. Wilde submitted a four-act play but was told that he would have to cut it to three acts so that it might be preceded by a one-act curtain-raiser, Langdon E. Mitchell's *In the Season,* a work of no lasting interest. Wilde made the necessary cuts, principally by condensing his original second and third acts into one, which is the second act of the play as it now stands. The principal omission is the scene in which a solicitor turns up to demand payment of debts incurred by "Ernest" in London. The debts are Jack's, but, in the country, Algernon is pretending to be Ernest, and he faces imprisonment because he will not give up his masquerade. The original four-act version was translated into German as *Ernst Sein!* An English reconstruction of it was edited by Wilde's son, Vyvyan Holland, in 1957. The year before, the New York Public Library published a four-act version based on Wilde's early drafts. In addition to the episode of the solicitor, Mr. Gribsby, the New York Public Library text has other distinctive features: a screen scene in which Algernon and Cecily hide from Lady Bracknell (who is here named Lady Brancaster), numerous opportunities for Algernon to consume more food (including one lunch of pâté and champagne and another of six lobsters), and an explanation for the complaint Miss Prism voices when she makes her last entrance in the play: "I was told you expected me in the vestry, dear Canon. I have been waiting for you there for an hour and three-quarters." In the New York Public Library text, Cecily gets rid of Miss Prism by telling her that Canon Chasuble will meet her in the vestry; Cecily's speech is omitted in the final version, but Miss Prism waits in the vestry nevertheless.

The reception of *The Importance of Being Earnest* was generally favorable, even though George Bernard Shaw, writing in the *Saturday Review,* found it "heartless"; as a farce—or, as Wilde chose to call it "farcical comedy"—it is, by definition, heartless. It disappeared from the stage in the years immediately following Wilde's disgrace, but, with the passing of time, it has become established as a universal favorite.

Henry Popkin

The Importance of
Being Earnest

A Trivial Comedy for Serious People

by OSCAR WILDE

THE PERSONS OF THE PLAY

John Worthing, J.P.
Algernon Moncrieff
Rev. Canon Chasuble, D.D.
Merriman, Butler
Lane, Manservant
Lady Bracknell
Hon. Gwendolen Fairfax
Cecily Cardew
Miss Prism, Governess

To
Robert Baldwin Ross
in appreciation
and
affection

THE SCENES OF THE PLAY

ACT I
Algernon Moncrieff's flat in Half-Moon Street, W.

ACT II
The garden at the Manor House, Woolton

ACT III
Drawing-room at the Manor House, Woolton

TIME
The Present

FIRST ACT

SCENE

Morning-room in ALGERNON's flat in Half-Moon Street. The room is luxuriously and artistically furnished. The sound of a piano is heard in the adjoining room.

(LANE is arranging afternoon tea on the table and, after the music has ceased, ALGERNON enters.)

Algernon.
Did you hear what I was playing, Lane?

Lane.
I didn't think it polite to listen, sir.

Algernon.
I'm sorry for that, for your sake. I don't play accurately—anyone can play accurately—but I play with wonderful expression. As far as the piano is concerned, sentiment is my forte. I keep science for Life.

Lane.
Yes, sir.

Algernon.
And, speaking of the science of Life, have you got the cucumber sandwiches cut for Lady Bracknell?

Lane.
Yes, sir. *(Hands them on a salver.)*

Algernon.
(Inspects them, takes two, and sits down on the sofa.) Oh! . . . by the way, Lane, I see from your book that on Thursday night, when Lord Shoreman and Mr

27

Worthing were dining with me, eight bottles of champagne are entered as having been consumed.

Lane.
Yes, sir; eight bottles and a pint.

Algernon.
Why is it that at a bachelor's establishment the servants invariably drink the champagne? I ask merely for information.

Lane.
I attribute it to the superior quality of the wine, sir. I have often observed that in married households the champagne is rarely of a first-rate brand.

Algernon.
Good heavens! Is marriage so demoralizing as that?

Lane.
I believe it *is* a very pleasant state, sir. I have had very little experience of it myself up to the present. I have only been married once. That was in consequence of a misunderstanding between myself and a young person.

Algernon.
(*Languidly.*) I don't know that I am much interested in your family life, Lane.

Lane.
No, sir; it is not a very interesting subject. I never think of it myself.

Algernon.
Very natural, I am sure. That will do, Lane, thank you.

Lane.
Thank you, sir.

(LANE *goes out.*)

Algernon.
Lane's views on marriage seem somewhat lax. Really, if the lower orders don't set us a good example, what on earth is the use of them? They seem, as a class, to have absolutely no sense of moral responsibility.

(*Enter* LANE.)

Lane.
Mr Ernest Worthing.

(*Enter* JACK. LANE *goes out.*)

Algernon.
How are you, my dear Ernest? What brings you up to town?

Jack.
Oh, pleasure, pleasure! What else should bring one anywhere? Eating as usual, I see, Algy!

Algernon.
(*Stiffly.*) I believe it is customary in good society to take some slight refreshment at five o'clock. Where have you been since last Thursday?

Jack.
(*Sitting down on the sofa.*) In the country.

Algernon.
What on earth do you do there?

Jack.
(*Pulling off his gloves.*) When one is in town one amuses oneself. When one is in the country one amuses other people. It is excessively boring.

Algernon.
And who are the people you amuse?

Jack.
(*Airily.*) Oh, neighbours, neighbours.

Algernon.
Got nice neighbours in your part of Shropshire?

Jack.
Perfectly horrid! Never speak to one of them.

Algernon.
How immensely you must amuse them! (*Goes over and takes sandwich.*) By the way, Shropshire is your county, is it not?

Jack.
Eh? Shropshire? Yes, of course. Hallo! Why all these cups? Why cucumber sandwiches? Why such reckless extravagance in one so young? Who is coming to tea?

Algernon.
Oh! merely Aunt Augusta and Gwendolen.

Jack.
How perfectly delightful!

Algernon.
Yes, that is all very well; but I am afraid Aunt Augusta won't quite approve of your being here.

Jack.
May I ask why?

Algernon.
My dear fellow, the way you flirt with Gwendolen is perfectly disgraceful. It is almost as bad as the way Gwendolen flirts with you.

Jack.
I am in love with Gwendolen. I have come up to town expressly to propose to her.

Algernon.
I thought you had come up for pleasure? ... I call that business.

Jack.
How utterly unromantic you are!

Algernon.
I really don't see anything romantic in proposing. It is very romantic to be in love. But there is nothing romantic about a definite proposal. Why, one may be accepted. One usually is, I believe. Then the excitement is all over. The very essence of romance is uncertainty. If ever I get married, I'll certainly try to forget the fact.

Jack.
I have no doubt about that, dear Algy. The Divorce Court was specially invented for people whose memories are so curiously constituted.

Algernon.
Oh, there is no use speculating on that subject. Divorces are made in Heaven—(JACK *puts out his hand to take a sandwich.* ALGERNON *at once interferes.*) Please don't touch the cucumber sandwiches. They are ordered specially for Aunt Augusta. (*Takes one and eats it.*)

Jack.
Well, you have been eating them all the time.

Algernon.
That is quite a different matter. She is my aunt. (*Takes plate from below.*) Have some bread and butter. The bread and butter is for Gwendolen. Gwendolen is devoted to bread and butter.

Jack.
(*Advancing to table and helping himself.*) And very good bread and butter it is too.

Algernon.
Well, my dear fellow, you need not eat as if you

were going to eat it all. You behave as if you were married to her already. You are not married to her already, and I don't think you ever will be.

Jack.
Why on earth do you say that?

Algernon.
Well, in the first place, girls never marry the men they flirt with. Girls don't think it right.

Jack.
Oh, that is nonsense!

Algernon.
It isn't. It is a great truth. It accounts for the extraordinary number of bachelors that one sees all over the place. In the second place, I don't give my consent.

Jack.
Your consent!

Algernon.
My dear fellow, Gwendolen is my first cousin. And before I allow you to marry her, you will have to clear up the whole question of Cecily. (*Rings bell.*)

Jack.
Cecily! What on earth do you mean? What do you mean, Algy, by Cecily! I don't know any one of the name of Cecily.

(*Enter* LANE.)

Algernon.
Bring me that cigarette case Mr Worthing left in the smoking-room the last time he dined here.

Lane.
Yes, sir.

(LANE *goes out.*)

Jack.
Do you mean to say you have had my cigarette case all this time? I wish to goodness you had let me know. I have been writing frantic letters to Scotland Yard about it. I was very nearly offering a large reward.

Algernon.
Well, I wish you would offer one. I happen to be more than usually hard up.

Jack.

There is no good offering a large reward now that the thing is found.

(*Enter* LANE *with the cigarette case on a salver.* ALGERNON *takes it at once.* LANE *goes out.*)

Algernon.

I think that is rather mean of you, Ernest, I must say. (*Opens case and examines it.*) However, it makes no matter, for, now that I look at the inscription inside, I find that the thing isn't yours after all.

Jack.

Of course it's mine. (*Moving to him.*) You have seen me with it a hundred times, and you have no right whatsoever to read what is written inside. It is a very ungentlemanly thing to read a private cigarette case.

Algernon.

Oh! it is absurd to have a hard and fast rule about what one should read and what one shouldn't. More than half of modern culture depends on what one shouldn't read.

Jack.

I am quite aware of the fact, and I don't propose to discuss modern culture. It isn't the sort of thing one should talk of in private. I simply want my cigarette case back.

Algernon.

Yes; but this isn't your cigarette case. This cigarette case is a present from someone of the name of Cecily, and you said you didn't know anyone of that name.

Jack.

Well, if you want to know, Cecily happens to be my aunt.

Algernon.

Your aunt!

Jack.

Yes. Charming old lady she is, too. Lives at Tunbridge Wells. Just give it back to me, Algy.

Algernon.

(*Retreating to back of sofa.*) But why does she call herself little Cecily if she is your aunt and lives at Tunbridge Wells? (*Reading.*) 'From little Cecily with her fondest love.'

Jack.
(*Moving to sofa and kneeling upon it.*) My dear fellow, what on earth is there in that? Some aunts are tall, some aunts are not tall. That is a matter that surely an aunt may be allowed to decide for herself. You seem to think that every aunt should be exactly like your aunt! That is absurd. For Heaven's sake give me back my cigarette case. (*Follows* ALGERNON *round the room.*)

Algernon.
Yes. But why does your aunt call you her uncle? 'From little Cecily, with her fondest love to her dear Uncle Jack.' There is no objection, I admit, to an aunt being a small aunt, but why an aunt, no matter what her size may be, should call her own nephew her uncle, I can't quite make out. Besides, your name isn't Jack at all; it is Ernest.

Jack.
It isn't Ernest; it's Jack.

Algernon.
You have always told me it was Ernest. I have introduced you to every one as Ernest. You answer to the name of Ernest. You look as if your name was Ernest. You are the most earnest-looking person I ever saw in my life. It is perfectly absurd your saying that your name isn't Ernest. It's on your cards. Here is one of them. (*Taking it from case.*) 'Mr Ernest Worthing, B.4, The Albany.' I'll keep this as a proof that your name is Ernest if ever you attempt to deny it to me, or to Gwendolen, or to anyone else. (*Puts the card in his pocket.*)

Jack.
Well, my name is Ernest in town and Jack in the country, and the cigarette case was given to me in the country.

Algernon.
Yes, but that does not account for the fact that your small Aunt Cecily, who lives at Tunbridge Wells, calls you her dear uncle. Come, old boy, you had much better have the thing out at once.

Jack.
My dear Algy, you talk exactly as if you were a den-

tist. It is very vulgar to talk like a dentist when one isn't a dentist. It produces a false impression.

Algernon.
Well, that is exactly what dentists always do. Now, go on! Tell me the whole thing. I may mention that I have always suspected you of being a confirmed and secret Bunburyist; and I am quite sure of it now.

Jack.
Bunburyist? What on earth do you mean by a Bunburyist?

Algernon.
I'll reveal to you the meaning of that incomparable expression as soon as you are kind enough to inform me why you are Ernest in town and Jack in the country.

Jack.
Well, produce my cigarette case first.

Algernon.
Here it is. (*Hands cigarette case.*) Now produce your explanation, and pray make it improbable. (*Sits on sofa.*)

Jack.
My dear fellow, there is nothing improbable about my explanation at all. In fact it's perfectly ordinary. Old Mr Thomas Cardew, who adopted me when I was a little boy, made me in his will guardian to his granddaughter, Miss Cecily Cardew. Cecily, who addresses me as her uncle from motives of respect that you could not possibly appreciate, lives at my place in the country under the charge of her admirable governess, Miss Prism.

Algernon.
Where is that place in the country, by the way?

Jack.
That is nothing to you, dear boy. You are not going to be invited. . . . I may tell you candidly that the place is not in Shropshire.

Algernon.
I suspected that, my dear fellow! I have Bunburyed all over Shropshire on two separate occasions. Now, go on. Why are you Ernest in town and Jack in the country?

Jack.
My dear Algy, I don't know whether you will be able
to understand my real motives. You are hardly serious
enough. When one is placed in the position of guardian, one has to adopt a very high moral tone on all
subjects. It's one's duty to do so. And as a high
moral tone can hardly be said to conduce very much
to either one's health or one's happiness, in order to
get up to town I have always pretended to have a
younger brother of the name of Ernest, who lives in
the Albany, and gets into the most dreadful scrapes.
That, my dear Algy, is the whole truth pure and
simple.

Algernon.
The truth is rarely pure and never simple. Modern
life would be very tedious if it were either, and modern
literature a complete impossibility!

Jack.
That wouldn't be at all a bad thing.

Algernon.
Literary criticism is not your forte, my dear fellow.
Don't try it. You should leave that to people who
haven't been at a University. They do it so well in
the daily papers. What you really are is a Bunburyist.
I was quite right in saying you were a Bunburyist.
You are one of the most advanced Bunburyists I know.

Jack.
What on earth do you mean?

Algernon.
You have invented a very useful younger brother
called Ernest, in order that you may be able to come
up to town as often as you like. I have invented an
invaluable permanent invalid called Bunbury, in order
that I may be able to go down into the country whenever I choose. Bunbury is perfectly invaluable. If it
wasn't for Bunbury's extraordinary bad health, for
instance, I wouldn't be able to dine with you at Willis's to-night, for I have been really engaged to Aunt
Augusta for more than a week.

Jack.
I haven't asked you to dine with me anywhere to-night.

Algernon.

I know. You are absurdly careless about sending out invitations. It is very foolish of you. Nothing annoys people so much as not receiving invitations.

Jack.

You had much better dine with your Aunt Augusta.

Algernon.

I haven't the smallest intention of doing anything of the kind. To begin with, I dined there on Monday, and once a week is quite enough to dine with one's own relations. In the second place, whenever I do dine there I am always treated as a member of the family, and sent down with either no woman at all, or two. In the third place, I know perfectly well whom she will place me next to, to-night. She will place me next Mary Farquhar, who always flirts with her own husband across the dinner-table. That is not very pleasant. Indeed, it is not even decent . . . and that sort of thing is enormously on the increase. The amount of women in London who flirt with their own husbands is perfectly scandalous. It looks so bad. It is simply washing one's clean linen in public. Besides, now that I know you to be a confirmed Bunburyist I naturally want to talk to you about Bunburying. I want to tell you the rules.

Jack.

I'm not a Bunburyist at all. If Gwendolen accepts me, I am going to kill my brother, indeed I think I'll kill him in any case. Cecily is a little too much interested in him. It is rather a bore. So I am going to get rid of Ernest. And I strongly advise you to do the same with Mr . . . with your invalid friend who has the absurd name.

Algernon.

Nothing will induce me to part with Bunbury, and if you ever get married, which seems to me extremely problematic, you will be very glad to know Bunbury. A man who marries without knowing Bunbury has a very tedious time of it.

Jack.

That is nonsense. If I marry a charming girl like

Gwendolen, and she is the only girl I ever saw in my life that I would marry, I certainly won't want to know Bunbury.

Algernon.
Then your wife will. You don't seem to realize, that in married life three is company and two is none.

Jack.
(*Sententiously.*) That, my dear young friend, is the theory that the corrupt French Drama has been propounding for the last fifty years.

Algernon.
Yes; and that the happy English home has proved in half the time.

Jack.
For heaven's sake, don't try to be cynical. It's perfectly easy to be cynical.

Algernon.
My dear fellow, it isn't easy to be anything nowadays. There's such a lot of beastly competition about. (*The sound of an electric bell is heard.*) Ah! that must be Aunt Augusta. Only relatives, or creditors, ever ring in that Wagnerian manner. Now, if I get her out of the way for ten minutes, so that you can have an opportunity for proposing to Gwendolen, may I dine with you tonight at Willis's?

Jack.
I suppose so, if you want to.

Algernon.
Yes, but you must be serious about it. I hate people who are not serious about meals. It is so shallow of them.

(*Enter* LANE.)

Lane.
Lady Bracknell and Miss Fairfax.

(ALGERNON *goes forward to meet them. Enter* LADY BRACKNELL *and* GWENDOLEN.)

Lady Bracknell.
Good afternoon, dear Algernon, I hope you are behaving very well.

Algernon.
I'm feeling very well, Aunt Augusta.

Lady Bracknell.
That's not quite the same thing. In fact the two things rarely go together. (*Sees* JACK *and bows to him with icy coldness.*)

Algernon.
(*To* GWENDOLEN.) Dear me, you are smart!

Gwendolen.
I am always smart! Am I not, Mr Worthing?

Jack.
You're quite perfect, Miss Fairfax.

Gwendolen.
Oh! I hope I am not that. It would leave no room for developments, and I intend to develop in many directions. (GWENDOLEN *and* JACK *sit down together in the corner.*)

Lady Bracknell.
I'm sorry if we are a little late, Algernon, but I was obliged to call on dear Lady Harbury. I hadn't been there since her poor husband's death. I never saw a woman so altered; she looks quite twenty years younger. And now I'll have a cup of tea, and one of those nice cucumber sandwiches you promised me.

Algernon.
Certainly, Aunt Augusta. (*Goes over to tea-table.*)

Lady Bracknell.
Won't you come and sit here, Gwendolen?

Gwendolen.
Thanks, mamma, I'm quite comfortable where I am.

Algernon.
(*Picking up empty plate in horror.*) Good heavens! Lane! Why are there no cucumber sandwiches? I ordered them specially.

Lane.
(*Gravely.*) There were no cucumbers in the market this morning, sir. I went down twice.

Algernon.
No cucumbers!

Lane.
No, sir. Not even for ready money.

Algernon.
That will do, Lane, thank you.

Lane.
Thank you, sir. (*Goes out.*)

Algernon.
I am greatly distressed, Aunt Augusta, about there being no cucumbers, not even for ready money.

Lady Bracknell.
It really makes no matter, Algernon. I had some crumpets with Lady Harbury, who seems to me to be living entirely for pleasure now.

Algernon.
I hear her hair has turned quite gold from grief.

Lady Bracknell.
It certainly has changed its colour. From what cause I, of course, cannot say. (ALGERNON *crosses and hands tea.*) Thank you, I've quite a treat for you tonight, Algernon. I am going to send you down with Mary Farquhar. She is such a nice woman, and so attentive to her husband. It's delightful to watch them.

Algernon.
I am afraid, Aunt Augusta, I shall have to give up the pleasure of dining with you tonight after all.

Lady Bracknell.
(*Frowning.*) I hope not, Algernon. It would put my table completely out. Your uncle would have to dine upstairs. Fortunately he is accustomed to that.

Algernon.
It is a great bore, and, I need hardly say, a terrible disappointment to me, but the fact is I have just had a telegram to say that my poor friend Bunbury is very ill again. (*Exchanges glances with* JACK.) They seem to think I should be with him.

Lady Bracknell.
It is very strange. This Mr Bunbury seems to suffer from curiously bad health.

Algernon.
Yes; poor Bunbury is a dreadful invalid.

Lady Bracknell.
Well, I must say, Algernon, that I think it is high time that Mr Bunbury made up his mind whether he was going to live or to die. This shilly-shallying with the question is absurd. Nor do I in any way approve of the modern sympathy with invalids. I consider it morbid. Illness of any kind is hardly a thing to be encouraged in others. Health is the primary duty of

life. I am always telling that to your poor uncle, but he never seems to take much notice ... as far as any improvement in his ailment goes. I should be much obliged if you would ask Mr Bunbury, from me, to be kind enough not to have a relapse on Saturday, for I rely on you to arrange my music for me. It is my last reception, and one wants something that will encourage conversation, particularly at the end of the season when everyone has practically said whatever they had to say, which, in most cases, was probably not much.

Algernon.

I'll speak to Bunbury, Aunt Augusta, if he is still conscious, and I think I can promise you he'll be all right by Saturday. Of course the music is a great difficulty. You see, if one plays good music, people don't listen, and if one plays bad music people don't talk. But I'll run over the programme I've drawn out, if you will kindly come into the next room for a moment.

Lady Bracknell.

Thank you, Algernon. It is very thoughtful of you. (*Rising, and following* ALGERNON.) I'm sure the programme will be delightful, after a few expurgations. French songs I cannot possibly allow. People always seem to think that they are improper, and either look shocked, which is vulgar, or laugh, which is worse. But German sounds a thoroughly respectable language, and, indeed I believe is so. Gwendolen, you will accompany me.

Gwendolen.

Certainly, mamma.

(LADY BRACKNELL *and* ALGERNON *go into the music-room,* GWENDOLEN *remains behind.*)

Jack.

Charming day it has been, Miss Fairfax.

Gwendolen.

Pray don't talk to me about the weather, Mr Worthing. Whenever people talk to me about the weather,

I always feel quite certain that they mean something else. And that makes me so nervous.

Jack.
I do mean something else.

Gwendolen.
I thought so. In fact, I am never wrong.

Jack.
And I would like to be allowed to take advantage of Lady Bracknell's temporary absence. . . .

Gwendolen.
I would certainly advise you to do so. Mamma has a way of coming back suddenly into a room that I have often had to speak to her about.

Jack.
(*Nervously.*) Miss Fairfax, ever since I met you I have admired you more than any girl . . . I have ever met since . . . I met you.

Gwendolen.
Yes, I am quite well aware of the fact. And I often wish that in public, at any rate, you had been more demonstrative. For me you have always had an irresistible fascination. Even before I met you I was far from indifferent to you. (JACK *looks at her in amazement.*) We live, as I hope you know, Mr Worthing, in an age of ideals. The fact is constantly mentioned in the more expensive monthly magazines, and has reached the provincial pulpits, I am told; and my ideal has always been to love someone of the name of Ernest. There is something in that name that inspires absolute confidence. The moment Algernon first mentioned to me that he had a friend called Ernest, I knew I was destined to love you.

Jack.
You really love me, Gwendolen?

Gwendolen.
Passionately!

Jack.
Darling! You don't know how happy you've made me.

Gwendolen.
My own Ernest!

Jack.

But you don't really mean to say that you couldn't love me if my name wasn't Ernest?

Gwendolen.

But your name is Ernest.

Jack.

Yes, I know it is. But supposing it was something else? Do you mean to say you couldn't love me then?

Gwendolen.

(*Glibly.*) Ah! that is clearly a metaphysical speculation, and like most metaphysical speculations has very little reference at all to the actual facts of real life, as we know them.

Jack.

Personally, darling, to speak quite candidly, I don't much care about the name of Ernest. . . . I don't think the name suits me at all.

Gwendolen.

It suits you perfectly. It is a divine name. It has music of its own. It produces vibrations.

Jack.

Well, really, Gwendolen, I must say that I think there are lots of other much nicer names. I think Jack, for instance, a charming name.

Gwendolen.

Jack? . . . No, there is very little music in the name Jack, if any at all, indeed. It does not thrill. It produces absolutely no vibrations. . . . I have known several Jacks, and they all, without exception, were more than usually plain. Besides, Jack is a notorious domesticity for John! And I pity any woman who is married to a man called John. She would probably never be allowed to know the entrancing pleasure of a single moment's solitude. The only really safe name is Ernest.

Jack.

Gwendolen, I must get christened at once—I mean we must get married at once. There is no time to be lost.

Gwendolen.

Married, Mr Worthing?

Jack.

(*Astounded.*) Well . . . surely. You know that I

love you, and you led me to believe, Miss Fairfax,
that you were not absolutely indifferent to me.

Gwendolen.
I adore you. But you haven't proposed to me yet.
Nothing has been said at all about marriage. The
subject has not even been touched on.

Jack.
Well . . . may I propose to you now?

Gwendolen.
I think it would be an admirable opportunity. And
to spare you any possible disappointment, Mr
Worthing, I think it only fair to tell you quite
frankly beforehand that I am fully determined to
accept you.

Jack.
Gwendolen!

Gwendolen.
Yes, Mr Worthing, what have you got to say to
me?

Jack.
You know what I have got to say to you.

Gwendolen.
Yes, but you don't say it.

Jack.
Gwendolen, will you marry me? (*Goes on his
knees.*)

Gwendolen.
Of course I will, darling. How long you have been
about it! I am afraid you have had very little experience in how to propose.

Jack.
My own one, I have never loved any one in the
world but you.

Gwendolen.
Yes, but men often propose for practice. I know
my brother Gerald does. All my girl-friends tell
me so. What wonderfully blue eyes you have,
Ernest! They are quite, quite blue. I hope you will
always look at me just like that, especially when
there are other people present.

(*Enter* LADY BRACKNELL.)

Lady Bracknell.
Mr Worthing! Rise, sir, from this semirecumbent posture. It is most indecorous.

Gwendolen.
Mamma! (*He tries to rise; she restrains him.*) I must beg you to retire. This is no place for you. Besides, Mr Worthing has not quite finished yet.

Lady Bracknell.
Finished what, may I ask?

Gwendolen.
I am engaged to Mr Worthing, mamma. (*They rise together.*)

Lady Bracknell.
Pardon me, you are not engaged to any one. When you do become engaged to some one, I, or your father, should his health permit him, will inform you of the fact. An engagement should come on a young girl as a surprise, pleasant or unpleasant, as the case may be. It is hardly a matter that she could be allowed to arrange for herself.... And now I have a few questions to put to you, Mr Worthing. While I am making these inquiries, you, Gwendolen, will wait for me below in the carriage.

Gwendolen.
(*Reproachfully.*) Mamma!

Lady Bracknell.
In the carriage, Gwendolen! (GWENDOLEN *goes to the door. She and* JACK *blow kisses to each other behind* LADY BRACKNELL's *back.* LADY BRACKNELL *looks vaguely about as if she could not understand what the noise was. Finally turns round.*) Gwendolen, the carriage!

Gwendolen.
Yes, mamma. (*Goes out, looking back at* JACK.)

Lady Bracknell.
(*Sitting down.*) You can take a seat, Mr Worthing.

(*Looks in her pocket for note-book and pencil.*)

Jack.
Thank you, Lady Bracknell, I prefer standing.

Lady Bracknell.
(*Pencil and note-book in hand.*) I feel bound to tell you that you are not down on my list of eligible young men, although I have the same list as the dear Duchess of Bolton has. We work together, in fact. However, I am quite ready to enter your name, should your answers be what a really affectionate mother requires. Do you smoke?

Jack.
Well, yes, I must admit I smoke.

Lady Bracknell.
I am glad to hear it. A man should always have an occupation of some kind. There are far too many idle men in London as it is. How old are you?

Jack.
Twenty-nine.

Lady Bracknell.
A very good age to be married at. I have always been of opinion that a man who desires to get married should know either everything or nothing. Which do you know?

Jack.
(*After some hesitation.*) I know nothing, Lady Bracknell.

Lady Bracknell.
I am pleased to hear it. I do not approve of anything that tampers with natural ignorance. Ignorance is like a delicate exotic fruit; touch it and the bloom is gone. The whole theory of modern education is radically unsound. Fortunately in England, at any rate, education produces no effect whatsoever. If it did, it would prove a serious danger to the upper classes, and probably lead to acts of violence in Grosvenor Square. What is your income?

Jack.
Between seven and eight thousand a year.

Lady Bracknell.
(*Makes a note in her book.*) In land, or in investments?

Jack.
In investments, chiefly.

Lady Bracknell.
That is satisfactory. What between the duties expected of one during one's lifetime, and the duties exacted from one after one's death, land has ceased to be either a profit or a pleasure. It gives one position, and prevents one from keeping it up. That's all that can be said about land.

Jack.
I have a country house with some land, of course, attached to it, about fifteen hundred acres, I believe; but I don't depend on that for my real income. In fact, as far as I can make out, the poachers are the only people who make anything out of it.

Lady Bracknell.
A country house! How many bedrooms? Well, that point can be cleared up afterwards. You have a town house, I hope? A girl with a simple, unspoiled nature, like Gwendolen, could hardly be expected to reside in the country.

Jack.
Well, I own a house in Belgrave Square, but it is let by the year to Lady Bloxham. Of course, I can get it back whenever I like, at six months' notice.

Lady Bracknell.
Lady Bloxham? I don't know her.

Jack.
Oh, she goes about very little. She is a lady considerably advanced in years.

Lady Bracknell.
Ah, nowadays that is no guarantee of respectability of character. What number in Belgrave Square?

Jack.
149.

Lady Bracknell.
(*Shaking her head.*) The unfashionable side. I thought there was something. However, that could easily be altered.

Jack.
Do you mean the fashion, or the side?

Lady Bracknell.
(*Sternly.*) Both, if necessary, I presume. What are your politics?

Jack.
Well, I am afraid I really have none. I am a Liberal Unionist.

Lady Bracknell.
Oh, they count as Tories. They dine with us. Or come in the evening, at any rate. Now to minor matters. Are your parents living?

Jack.
I have lost both my parents.

Lady Bracknell.
To lose one parent, Mr Worthing, may be regarded as a misfortune; to lose both looks like carelessness. Who was your father? He was evidently a man of some wealth. Was he born in what the Radical papers call the purple of commerce, or did he rise from the ranks of the aristocracy?

Jack.
I am afraid I really don't know. The fact is, Lady Bracknell, I said I had lost my parents. It would be nearer the truth to say that my parents seem to have lost me. . . . I don't actually know who I am by birth. I was . . . well, I was found.

Lady Bracknell.
Found!

Jack.
The late Mr Thomas Cardew, an old gentleman of a very charitable and kindly disposition, found me, and gave me the name of Worthing, because he happened to have a first-class ticket for Worthing in his pocket at the time. Worthing is a place in Sussex. It is a seaside resort.

Lady Bracknell.
Where did the charitable gentleman who had a first-class ticket for this seaside resort find you?

Jack.
(*Gravely.*) In a hand-bag.

Lady Bracknell.
A hand-bag?

Jack.
(*Very seriously.*) Yes, Lady Bracknell. I was in a hand-bag—a somewhat large, black leather hand-bag, with handles to it—an ordinary hand-bag in fact.

Lady Bracknell.
In what locality did this Mr James, or Thomas, Cardew come across this ordinary hand-bag?

Jack.
In the cloak-room at Victoria Station. It was given to him in mistake for his own.

Lady Bracknell.
The cloak-room at Victoria Station?

Jack.
Yes. The Brighton line.

Lady Bracknell.
The line is immaterial. Mr Worthing, I confess I feel somewhat bewildered by what you have just told me. To be born, or at any rate bred, in a hand-bag, whether it had handles or not, seems to me to display a contempt for the ordinary decencies of family life that reminds one of the worst excesses of the French Revolution. And I presume you know what that unfortunate movement led to? As for the particular locality in which the hand-bag was found, a cloak-room at a railway station might serve to conceal a social indiscretion——has probably, indeed, been used for that purpose before now——but it could hardly be regarded as an assured basis for a recognized position in good society.

Jack.
May I ask you then what you would advise me to do? I need hardly say I would do anything in the world to ensure Gwendolen's happiness.

Lady Bracknell.
I would strongly advise you, Mr Worthing, to try and acquire some relations as soon as possible, and to make a definite effort to produce at any rate one parent, of either sex, before the season is quite over.

Jack.
Well, I don't see how I could possibly manage to do that. I can produce the hand-bag at any moment. It is in my dressing-room at home. I really think that should satisfy you, Lady Bracknell.

Lady Bracknell.
Me, sir! What has it to do with me? You can hardly imagine that I and Lord Bracknell would dream
of allowing our only daughter—a girl brought up
with the utmost care—to marry into a cloak-room,
and form an alliance with a parcel. Good morning,
Mr Worthing!

(LADY BRACKNELL *sweeps out in majestic
indignation.*)

Jack.
Good morning! (ALGERNON, *from the other room,
strikes up the Wedding March. JACK looks perfectly furious, and goes to the door.*) For goodness' sake
don't play that ghastly tune, Algy! How idiotic you
are!

(*The music stops and* ALGERNON *enters
cheerily.*)

Algernon.
Didn't it go off all right, old boy? You don't mean
to say Gwendolen refused you? I know it is a way
she has. She is always refusing people. I think it
is most ill-natured of her.

Jack.
Oh, Gwendolen is as right as a trivet. As far as she
is concerned, we are engaged. Her mother is perfectly unbearable. Never met such a Gorgon.... I don't
really know what a Gorgon is like, but I am quite
sure that Lady Bracknell is one. In any case, she is
a monster, without being a myth, which is rather unfair.... I beg your pardon, Algy, I suppose I
shouldn't talk about your own aunt in that way before you.

Algernon.
My dear boy, I love hearing my relations abused. It
is the only thing that makes me put up with them
at all. Relations are simply a tedious pack of people,
who haven't got the remotest knowledge of how to
live, nor the smallest instinct about when to die.

Jack.
Oh, that is nonsense!

Algernon.
It isn't!

Jack.
Well, I won't argue about the matter. You always want to argue about things.

Algernon.
That is exactly what things were originally made for.

Jack.
Upon my word, if I thought that, I'd shoot myself. ... (*A pause.*) You don't think there is any chance of Gwendolen becoming like her mother in about a hundred and fifty years, do you, Algy?

Algernon.
All women become like their mothers. That is their tragedy. No man does. That's his.

Jack.
Is that clever?

Algernon.
It is perfectly phrased! and quite as true as any observation in civilized life should be.

Jack.
I am sick to death of cleverness. Everybody is clever nowadays. You can't go anywhere without meeting clever people. The thing has become an absolute public nuisance. I wish to goodness we had a few fools left.

Algernon.
We have.

Jack.
I should extremely like to meet them. What do they talk about?

Algernon.
The fools? Oh! about the clever people, of course.

Jack.
What fools.

Algernon.
By the way, did you tell Gwendolen the truth about your being Ernest in town, and Jack in the country?

Jack.
(*In a very patronizing manner.*) My dear fellow, the truth isn't quite the sort of thing one tells to a nice, sweet, refined girl. What extraordinary ideas you have about the way to behave to a woman!

Algernon.
The only way to behave to a woman is to make love to her, if she is pretty, and to someone else, if she is plain.

Jack.
Oh, that is nonsense.

Algernon.
What about your brother? What about the profligate Ernest?

Jack.
Oh, before the end of the week I shall have got rid of him. I'll say he died in Paris of apoplexy. Lots of people die of apoplexy, quite suddenly, don't they?

Algernon.
Yes, but it's hereditary, my dear fellow. It's a sort of thing that runs in families. You had much better say a severe chill.

Jack.
You are sure a severe chill isn't hereditary, or anything of that kind?

Algernon.
Of course it isn't!

Jack.
Very well, then. My poor brother Ernest is carried off suddenly, in Paris, by a severe chill. That gets rid of him.

Algernon.
But I thought you said that . . . Miss Cardew was a little too much interested in your poor brother Ernest? Won't she feel his loss a good deal?

Jack.
Oh, that is all right. Cecily is not a silly romantic girl, I am glad to say. She has got a capital appetite, goes long walks, and pays no attention at all to her lessons.

Algernon.
I would rather like to see Cecily.

Jack.
I will take very good care you never do. She is excessively pretty, and she is only just eighteen.

Algernon.
Have you told Gwendolen yet that you have an excessively pretty ward who is only just eighteen?

Jack.
Oh! one doesn't blurt these things out to people. Cecily and Gwendolen are perfectly certain to be extremely great friends. I'll bet you anything you like that half an hour after they have met, they will be calling each other sister.

Algernon.
Women only do that when they have called each other a lot of other things first. Now, my dear boy, if we want to get a good table at Willis's, we really must go and dress. Do you know it is nearly seven?

Jack.
(*Irritably.*) Oh! it always is nearly seven.

Algernon.
I'm hungry.

Jack.
I never knew you when you weren't. . . .

Algernon.
What shall we do after dinner? Go to a theatre?

Jack.
Oh, no! I loathe listening.

Algernon.
Well, let us go to the Club?

Jack.
Oh, no! I hate talking.

Algernon.
Well, we might trot round to the Empire at ten?

Jack.
Oh, no! I can't bear looking at things. It is so silly.

Algernon.
Well, what shall we do?

Jack.
Nothing!

Algernon.
It is awfully hard work doing nothing. However, I don't mind hard work where there is no definite object of any kind.

(*Enter* LANE.)

Lane.
Miss Fairfax.

(*Enter* GWENDOLEN. LANE *goes out.*)

Algernon.
Gwendolen, upon my word!

Gwendolen.
Algy, kindly turn your back. I have something very particular to say to Mr Worthing.

Algernon.
Really, Gwendolen, I don't think I can allow this at all.

Gwendolen.
Algy, you always adopt a strictly immoral attitude towards life. You are not quite old enough to do that. (ALGERNON *retires to the fireplace.*)

Jack.
My own darling!

Gwendolen.
Ernest, we may never be married. From the expression on mamma's face I fear we never shall. Few parents nowadays pay any regard to what their children say to them. The old-fashioned respect for the young is fast dying out. Whatever influence I ever had over mamma, I lost at the age of three. But although she may prevent us from becoming man and wife, and I may marry someone else, and marry often, nothing that she can possibly do can alter my eternal devotion to you.

Jack.
Dear Gwendolen!

Gwendolen.
The story of your romantic origin, as related to me by mamma, with unpleasing comments, has naturally stirred the deeper fibres of my nature. Your Christian name has an irresistible fascination. The simplicity of your character makes you exquisitely incomprehensible to me. Your town address at the Albany I have. What is your address in the country?

Jack.
The Manor House, Woolton, Hertfordshire.

(ALGERNON, *who has been carefully listening, smiles to himself, and writes the address on his shirt-cuff. Then picks up the Railway Guide.*)

Gwendolen.
There is a good postal service, I suppose? It may be

necessary to do something desperate. That of course will require serious consideration. I will communicate with you daily.

Jack.
My own one!

Gwendolen.
How long do you remain in town?

Jack.
Till Monday.

Gwendolen.
Good! Algy, you may turn round now.

Algernon.
Thanks, I've turned round already.

Gwendolen.
You may also ring the bell.

Jack.
You will let me see you to your carriage, my own darling?

Gwendolen.
Certainly.

Jack.
(*To* LANE, *who now enters.*) I will see Miss Fairfax out.

Lane.
Yes, sir. (JACK *and* GWENDOLEN *go off.*)

(LANE *presents several letters on a salver, to* ALGERNON. *It is to be surmised that they are bills, as* ALGERNON, *after looking at the envelopes, tears them up.*)

Algernon.
A glass of sherry, Lane.

Lane.
Yes, sir.

Algernon.
Tomorrow, Lane, I'm going Bunburying.

Lane.
Yes, sir.

Algernon.
I shall probably not be back till Monday. You can put up my dress clothes, my smoking jacket, and all the Bunbury suits . . .

Lane.
Yes, sir. (*Handing sherry.*)

Algernon.
I hope tomorrow will be a fine day, Lane.

Lane.
It never is, sir.

Algernon.
Lane, you're a perfect pessimist.

Lane.
I do my best to give satisfaction, sir.

(*Enter* JACK. LANE *goes off.*)

Jack.
There's a sensible, intellectual girl! the only girl I ever cared for in my life. (ALGERNON *is laughing immoderately.*) What on earth are you so amused at?

Algernon.
Oh, I'm a little anxious about poor Bunbury, that is all.

Jack.
If you don't take care, your friend Bunbury will get you into a serious scrape some day.

Algernon.
I love scrapes. They are the only things that are never serious.

Jack.
Oh, that's nonsense, Algy. You never talk anything but nonsense.

Algernon.
Nobody ever does.

(JACK *looks indignantly at him, and leaves the room.* ALGERNON *lights a cigarette, reads his shirt-cuff, and smiles.*)

ACT DROP

SECOND ACT

SCENE

Garden at the Manor House. A flight of grey stone steps leads up to the house. The garden, an old-fashioned one, full of roses. Time of year, July. Basket chairs, and a table covered with books, are set under a large yew-tree.

(MISS PRISM *discovered seated at the table.* CECILY *is at the back, watering flowers.*)

Miss Prism.
(*Calling.*) Cecily, Cecily! Surely such a utilitarian occupation as the watering of flowers is rather Moulton's duty than yours? Especially at a moment when intellectual pleasures await you. Your German grammar is on the table. Pray open it at page fifteen. We will repeat yesterday's lesson.

Cecily.
(*Coming over very slowly.*) But I don't like German. It isn't at all a becoming language. I know perfectly well that I look quite plain after my German lesson.

Miss Prism.
Child, you know how anxious your guardian is that you should improve yourself in every way. He laid particular stress on your German, as he was leaving for town yesterday. Indeed, he always lays stress on your German when he is leaving for town.

Cecily.
Dear Uncle Jack is so very serious! Sometimes he is so serious that I think he cannot be quite well.

56

Miss Prism.
(*Drawing herself up.*) Your guardian enjoys the best of health, and his gravity of demeanour is especially to be commended in one so comparatively young as he is. I know no one who has a higher sense of duty and responsibility.

Cecily.
I suppose that is why he often looks a little bored when we three are together.

Miss Prism.
Cecily! I am surprised at you. Mr Worthing has many troubles in his life. Idle merriment and triviality would be out of place in his conversation. You must remember his constant anxiety about that unfortunate young man his brother.

Cecily.
I wish Uncle Jack would allow that unfortunate young man, his brother, to come down here sometimes. We might have a good influence over him, Miss Prism. I am sure you certainly would. You know German, and geology, and things of that kind influence a man very much. (CECILY *begins to write in her diary.*)

Miss Prism.
(*Shaking her head.*) I do not think that even I could produce any effect on a character that according to his own brother's admission is irretrievably weak and vacillating. Indeed I am not sure that I would desire to reclaim him. I am not in favour of this modern mania for turning bad people into good people at a moment's notice. As a man sows so let him reap. You must put away your diary, Cecily. I really don't see why you should keep a diary at all.

Cecily.
I keep a diary in order to enter the wonderful secrets of my life. If I didn't write them down, I should probably forget all about them.

Miss Prism.
Memory, my dear Cecily, is the diary that we all carry about with us.

Cecily.
Yes, but it usually chronicles the things that have never happened, and couldn't possibly have hap-

pened. I believe that Memory is responsible for nearly all the three-volume novels that Mudie sends us.

Miss Prism.
Do not speak slightingly of the three-volume novel, Cecily. I wrote one myself in earlier days.

Cecily.
Did you really, Miss Prism? How wonderfully clever you are! I hope it did not end happily? I don't like novels that end happily. They depress me so much.

Miss Prism.
The good ended happily, and the bad unhappily. That is what Fiction means.

Cecily.
I suppose so. But it seems very unfair. And was your novel ever published?

Miss Prism.
Alas! no. The manuscript unfortunately was abandoned. (CECILY *starts.*) I used the word in the sense of lost or mislaid. To your work, child, these speculations are profitless.

Cecily.
(*Smiling.*) But I see dear Dr Chasuble coming up through the garden.

Miss Prism.
(*Rising and advancing.*) Dr Chasuble! This is indeed a pleasure.

(*Enter* CANON CHASUBLE.)

Chasuble.
And how are we this morning? Miss Prism, you are, I trust, well?

Cecily.
Miss Prism has just been complaining of a slight headache. I think it would do her so much good to have a short stroll with you in the Park, Dr Chasuble.

Miss Prism.
Cecily, I have not mentioned anything about a headache.

Cecily.
No, dear Miss Prism, I know that, but I felt instinctively that you had a headache. Indeed I was thinking about that, and not about my German lesson, when the Rector came in.

Chasuble.
I hope, Cecily, you are not inattentive.

Cecily.
Oh, I am afraid I am.

Chasuble.
That is strange. Were I fortunate enough to be Miss Prism's pupil, I would hang upon her lips. (MISS PRISM *glares*.) I spoke metaphorically.—My metaphor was drawn from bees. Ahem! Mr Worthing, I suppose, has not returned from town yet?

Miss Prism.
We do not expect him till Monday afternoon.

Chasuble.
Ah yes, he usually likes to spend his Sunday in London. He is not one of those whose sole aim is enjoyment, as, by all accounts, that unfortunate young man his brother seems to be. But I must not disturb Egeria and her pupil any longer.

Miss Prism.
Egeria? My name is Laetitia, Doctor.

Chasuble.
(*Bowing.*) A classical allusion merely, drawn from the Pagan authors. I shall see you both no doubt at Evensong?

Miss Prism.
I think, dear Doctor, I will have a stroll with you. I find I have a headache after all, and a walk might do it good.

Chasuble.
With pleasure, Miss Prism, with pleasure. We might go as far as the schools and back.

Miss Prism.
That would be delightful. Cecily, you will read your Political Economy in my absence. The chapter on the Fall of the Rupee you may omit. It is somewhat too sensational. Even these metallic problems have their melodramatic side.

(*Goes down the garden with* DR CHASUBLE.)

Cecily.
(*Picks up books and throws them back on table.*) Horrid Political Economy! Horrid Geography! Horrid, horrid German!

(*Enter* MERRIMAN *with a card on a salver.*)

Merriman.
Mr Ernest Worthing has just driven over from the station. He has brought his luggage with him.

Cecily.
(*Takes the card and reads it.*) 'Mr Ernest Worthing, B.4, The Albany, W.' Uncle Jack's brother! Did you tell him Mr Worthing was in town?

Merriman.
Yes, Miss. He seemed very much disappointed. I mentioned that you and Miss Prism were in the garden. He said he was anxious to speak to you privately for a moment.

Cecily.
Ask Mr Ernest Worthing to come here. I suppose you had better talk to the housekeeper about a room for him.

Merriman.
Yes, Miss. (MERRIMAN *goes off.*)

Cecily.
I have never met any really wicked person before. I feel rather frightened. I am so afraid he will look just like every one else.

(*Enter* ALGERNON, *very gay and debonair.*)

He does!

Algernon.
(*Raising his hat.*) You are my little cousin Cecily, I'm sure.

Cecily.
You are under some strange mistake. I am not little. In fact, I believe I am more than usually tall for my age. (ALGERNON *is rather taken aback.*) But I am your cousin Cecily. You, I see from your card, are Uncle Jack's brother, my cousin Ernest, my wicked cousin Ernest.

Algernon.
Oh! I am not really wicked at all, Cousin Cecily. You mustn't think that I am wicked.

Cecily.
If you are not, then you have certainly been deceiving us all in a very inexcusable manner. I hope you

have not been leading a double life, pretending to be wicked and being really good all the time. That would be hypocrisy.

Algernon.
(*Looks at her in amazement.*) Oh! Of course I have been rather reckless.

Cecily.
I am glad to hear it.

Algernon.
In fact, now you mention the subject, I have been very bad in my own small way.

Cecily.
I don't think you should be so proud of that, though I am sure it must have been very pleasant.

Algernon.
It is much pleasanter being here with you.

Cecily.
I can't understand how you are here at all. Uncle Jack won't be back till Monday afternoon.

Algernon.
That is a great disappointment. I am obliged to go up by the first train on Monday morning. I have a business appointment that I am anxious . . . to miss!

Cecily.
Couldn't you miss it anywhere but in London?

Algernon.
No: the appointment is in London.

Cecily.
Well, I know, of course, how important it is not to keep a business engagement, if one wants to retain any sense of the beauty of life, but still I think you had better wait till Uncle Jack arrives. I know he wants to speak to you about your emigrating.

Algernon.
About my what?

Cecily.
Your emigrating. He has gone up to buy your outfit.

Algernon.
I certainly wouldn't let Jack buy my outfit. He has no taste in neckties at all.

Cecily.
I don't think you will require neckties. Uncle Jack is sending you to Australia.

Algernon.

Australia! I'd sooner die.

Cecily.

Well, he said at dinner on Wednesday night, that you would have to choose between this world, the next world, and Australia.

Algernon.

Oh, well! The accounts I have received of Australia and the next world are not particularly encouraging. This world is good enough for me, Cousin Cecily.

Cecily.

Yes, but are you good enough for it?

Algernon.

I'm afraid I'm not that. That is why I want you to reform me. You might make that your mission, if you don't mind, Cousin Cecily.

Cecily.

I'm afraid I've no time, this afternoon.

Algernon.

Well, would you mind my reforming myself this afternoon?

Cecily.

It is rather Quixotic of you. But I think you should try.

Algernon.

I will. I feel better already.

Cecily.

You are looking a little worse.

Algernon.

That is because I am hungry.

Cecily.

How thoughtless of me. I should have remembered that when one is going to lead an entirely new life, one requires regular and wholesome meals. Won't you come in?

Algernon.

Thank you. Might I have a buttonhole first? I have never any appetite unless I have a buttonhole first.

Cecily.

A Maréchal Niel? (*Picks up scissors.*)

Algernon.

No, I'd sooner have a pink rose.

Cecily.

Why? (*Cuts a flower.*)

Algernon.
Because you are like a pink rose, Cousin Cecily.

Cecily.
I don't think it can be right for you to talk to me like that. Miss Prism never says such things to me.

Algernon.
Then Miss Prism is a short-sighted old lady. (CECILY *puts the rose in his buttonhole.*) You are the prettiest girl I ever saw.

Cecily.
Miss Prism says that all good looks are a snare.

Algernon.
They are a snare that every sensible man would like to be caught in.

Cecily.
Oh, I don't think I would care to catch a sensible man. I shouldn't know what to talk to him about.

(*They pass into the house.* MISS PRISM *and* DR CHASUBLE *return.*)

Miss Prism.
You are too much alone, dear Dr Chasuble. You should get married. A misanthrope I can understand —a womanthrope, never!

Chasuble.
(*With a scholar's shudder.*) Believe me, I do not deserve so neologistic a phrase. The precept as well as the practice of the Primitive Church was distinctly against matrimony.

Miss Prism.
(*Sententiously.*) That is obviously the reason why the Primitive Church has not lasted up to the present day. And you do not seem to realize, dear Doctor, that by persistently remaining single, a man converts himself into a permanent public temptation. Men should be more careful; this very celibacy leads weaker vessels astray.

Chasuble.
But is a man not equally attractive when married?

Miss Prism.
No married man is ever attractive except to his wife.

Chasuble.
And often, I've been told, not even to her.

Miss Prism.
That depends on the intellectual sympathies of the woman. Maturity can always be depended on. Ripeness can be trusted. Young women are green. (DR CHASUBLE *starts.*) I spoke horticulturally. My metaphor was drawn from fruits. But where is Cecily?

Chasuble.
Perhaps she followed us to the schools.

(*Enter JACK slowly from the back of the garden. He is dressed in the deepest mourning, with crepe hatband and black gloves.*)

Miss Prism.
Mr Worthing!

Chasuble.
Mr Worthing?

Miss Prism.
This is indeed a surprise. We did not look for you till Monday afternoon.

Jack.
(*Shakes MISS PRISM's hand in a tragic manner.*) I have returned sooner than I expected. Dr Chasuble, I hope you are well?

Chasuble.
Dear Mr Worthing, I trust this garb of woe does not betoken some terrible calamity?

Jack.
My brother.

Miss Prism.
More shameful debts and extravagance?

Chasuble.
Still leading his life of pleasure?

Jack.
(*Shaking his head.*) Dead!

Chasuble.
Your brother Ernest dead?

Jack.
Quite dead.

Miss Prism.
What a lesson for him! I trust he will profit by it.

Chasuble.
Mr Worthing, I offer you my sincere condolence. You have at least the consolation of knowing that

you were always the most generous and forgiving of brothers.

Jack.
Poor Ernest! He had many faults, but it is a sad, sad blow.

Chasuble.
Very sad indeed. Were you with him at the end?

Jack.
No. He died abroad; in Paris, in fact. I had a telegram last night from the manager of the Grand Hotel.

Chasuble.
Was the cause of death mentioned?

Jack.
A severe chill, it seems.

Miss Prism.
As a man sows, so shall he reap.

Chasuble.
(*Raising his hand.*) Charity, dear Miss Prism, charity! None of us are perfect. I myself am peculiarly susceptible to draughts. Will the interment take place here?

Jack.
No. He seems to have expressed a desire to be buried in Paris.

Chasuble.
In Paris! (*Shakes his head.*) I fear that hardly points to any very serious state of mind at the last. You would no doubt wish me to make some slight allusion to this tragic domestic affliction next Sunday. (JACK *presses his hand convulsively.*) My sermon on the meaning of the manna in the wilderness can be adapted to almost any occasion, joyful, or, as in the present case, distressing. (*All sigh.*) I have preached it at harvest celebrations, christenings, confirmations, on days of humiliation and festal days. The last time I delivered it was in the Cathedral, as a charity sermon on behalf of the Society for the Prevention of Discontent among the Upper Orders. The Bishop, who was present, was much struck by some of the analogies I drew.

Jack.
Ah! that reminds me, you mentioned christenings I think, Dr Chasuble? I suppose you know how to

christen all right? (DR CHASUBLE *looks astounded.*) I mean, of course, you are continually christening, aren't you?

Miss Prism.
It is, I regret to say, one of the Rector's most constant duties in this parish. I have often spoken to the poorer classes on the subject. But they don't seem to know what thrift is.

Chasuble.
But is there any particular infant in whom you are interested, Mr Worthing? Your brother was, I believe, unmarried, was he not?

Jack.
Oh yes.

Miss Prism.
(*Bitterly.*) People who live entirely for pleasure usually are.

Jack.
But it is not for any child, dear Doctor. I am very fond of children. No! the fact is, I would like to be christened myself, this afternoon, if you have nothing better to do.

Chasuble.
But surely, Mr Worthing, you have been christened already?

Jack.
I don't remember anything about it.

Chasuble.
But have you any grave doubts on the subject?

Jack.
I certainly intend to have. Of course I don't know if the thing would bother you in any way, or if you think I am a little too old now.

Chasuble.
Not at all. The sprinkling, and, indeed, the immersion of adults is a perfectly canonical practice.

Jack.
Immersion!

Chasuble.
You need have no apprehensions. Sprinkling is all that is necessary, or indeed I think advisable. Our weather is so changeable. At what hour would you wish the ceremony performed?

Jack.

Oh, I might trot round about five if that would suit you.

Chasuble.

Perfectly, perfectly! In fact I have two similar ceremonies to perform at that time. A case of twins that occurred recently in one of the outlying cottages on your own estate. Poor Jenkins the carter, a most hard-working man.

Jack.

Oh! I don't see much fun in being christened along with other babies. It would be childish. Would half-past five do?

Chasuble.

Admirably! Admirably! (*Takes out watch.*) And now, dear Mr Worthing, I will not intrude any longer into a house of sorrow. I would merely beg you not to be too much bowed down by grief. What seem to us bitter trials are often blessings in disguise.

Miss Prism.

This seems to me a blessing of an extremely obvious kind.

(*Enter* CECILY *from the house.*)

Cecily.

Uncle Jack! Oh, I am pleased to see you back. But what horrid clothes you have got on. Do go and change them.

Miss Prism.

Cecily!

Chasuble.

My child! my child. (CECILY *goes towards* JACK; *he kisses her brow in a melancholy manner.*)

Cecily.

What is the matter, Uncle Jack? Do look happy! You look as if you had toothache, and I have got such a surprise for you. Who do you think is in the dining-room? Your brother!

Jack.

Who?

Cecily.

Your brother Ernest. He arrived about half an hour ago.

Jack.
What nonsense! I haven't got a brother.

Cecily.
Oh, don't say that. However badly he may have be-haved to you in the past he is still your brother. You couldn't be so heartless as to disown him. I'll tell him to come out. And you will shake hands with him, won't you, Uncle Jack? (*Runs back into the house.*)

Chasuble.
These are very joyful tidings.

Miss Prism.
After we had all been resigned to his loss, his sudden return seems to me peculiarly distressing.

Jack.
My brother is in the dining-room? I don't know what it all means. I think it is perfectly absurd.

(*Enter* ALGERNON *and* CECILY *hand in hand. They come slowly up to* JACK.)

Jack.
Good heavens! (*Motions* ALGERNON *away.*)

Algernon.
Brother John, I have come down from town to tell you that I am very sorry for all the trouble I have given you, and that I intend to lead a better life in the future. (JACK *glares at him and does not take his hand.*)

Cecily.
Uncle Jack, you are not going to refuse your own brother's hand?

Jack.
Nothing will induce me to take his hand. I think his coming down here disgraceful. He knows perfectly well why.

Cecily.
Uncle Jack, do be nice. There is some good in every-one. Ernest has just been telling me about his poor invalid friend Mr Bunbury whom he goes to visit so often. And surely there must be much good in one who is kind to an invalid, and leaves the pleasures of London to sit by a bed of pain.

Jack.
Oh! he has been talking about Bunbury, has he?

Cecily.
Yes, he has told me all about poor Mr Bunbury, and his terrible state of health.

Jack.
Bunbury! Well, I won't have him talk to you about Bunbury or about anything else. It is enough to drive one perfectly frantic.

Algernon.
Of course I admit that the faults were all on my side. But I must say that I think that Brother John's coldness to me is peculiarly painful. I expected a more enthusiastic welcome especially considering it is the first time I have come here.

Cecily.
Uncle Jack, if you don't shake hands with Ernest, I will never forgive you.

Jack.
Never forgive me?

Cecily.
Never, never, never!

Jack.
Well, this is the last time I shall ever do it. (*Shakes hands with* ALGERNON *and glares.*)

Chasuble.
It's pleasant, is it not, to see so perfect a reconciliation? I think we might leave the two brothers together.

Miss Prism.
Cecily, you will come with us.

Cecily.
Certainly, Miss Prism. My little task of reconciliation is over.

Chasuble.
You have done a beautiful action today, dear child.

Miss Prism.
We must not be premature in our judgements.

Cecily.
I feel very happy. (*They all go off except* JACK *and* ALGERNON.)

Jack.
You young scoundrel, Algy, you must get out of this

place as soon as possible. I don't allow any Bunburying here.

(*Enter* MERRIMAN.)

Merriman.
I have put Mr Ernest's things in the room next to
yours, sir. I suppose that is all right?

Jack.
What?

Merriman.
Mr Ernest's luggage, sir. I have unpacked it and put
it in the room next to your own.

Jack.
His luggage?

Merriman.
Yes, sir. Three portmanteaus, a dressing-case, two
hatboxes, and a large luncheon-basket.

Algernon.
I am afraid I can't stay more than a week this time.

Jack.
Merriman, order the dog-cart at once. Mr Ernest has
been suddenly called back to town.

Merriman.
Yes, sir. (*Goes back into the house.*)

Algernon.
What a fearful liar you are, Jack. I have not been
called back to town at all.

Jack.
Yes, you have.

Algernon.
I haven't heard any one call me.

Jack.
Your duty as a gentleman calls you back.

Algernon.
My duty as a gentleman has never interfered with
my pleasures in the smallest degree.

Jack.
I can quite understand that.

Algernon.
Well, Cecily is a darling.

Jack.
You are not to talk of Miss Cardew like that. I don't
like it.

Algernon.
Well, I don't like your clothes. You look perfectly

ridiculous in them. Why on earth don't you go up and change? It is perfectly childish to be in deep mourning for a man who is actually staying for a whole week with you in your house as a guest. I call it grotesque.

Jack.
You are certainly not staying with me for a whole week as a guest or anything else. You have got to leave . . . by the four-five train.

Algernon.
I certainly won't leave you so long as you are in mourning. It would be most unfriendly. If I were in mourning you would stay with me, I suppose. I should think it very unkind if you didn't.

Jack.
Well, will you go if I change my clothes?

Algernon.
Yes, if you are not too long. I never saw anybody take so long to dress, and with such little result.

Jack.
Well, at any rate, that is better than being always over-dressed as you are.

Algernon.
If I am occasionally a little over-dressed, I make up for it by being always immensely over-educated.

Jack.
Your vanity is ridiculous, your conduct an outrage, and your presence in my garden utterly absurd. However, you have got to catch the four-five, and I hope you will have a pleasant journey back to town. This Bunburying, as you call it, has not been a great success for you.

(*Goes into the house.*)

Algernon.
I think it has been a great success. I'm in love with Cecily, and that is everything.

(*Enter* CECILY *at the back of the garden. She picks up the can and begins to water the flowers.*)

But I must see her before I go, and make arrangements for another Bunbury. Ah, there she is.

Cecily.

Oh, I merely came back to water the roses. I thought you were with Uncle Jack.

Algernon.

He's gone to order the dog-cart for me.

Cecily.

Oh, is he going to take you for a nice drive?

Algernon.

He's going to send me away.

Cecily.

Then have we got to part?

Algernon.

I am afraid so. It's a very painful parting.

Cecily.

It is always painful to part from people whom one has known for a very brief space of time. The absence of old friends one can endure with equanimity. But even a momentary separation from any one to whom one has just been introduced is almost unbearable.

Algernon.

Thank you.

(Enter MERRIMAN.*)*

Merriman.

The dog-cart is at the door, sir.

(ALGERNON looks appealingly at CECILY.*)*

Cecily.

It can wait, Merriman . . . for . . . five minutes.

Merriman.

Yes, Miss.

(Exit MERRIMAN.*)*

Algernon.

I hope, Cecily, I shall not offend you if I state quite frankly and openly that you seem to me to be in every way the visible personification of absolute perfection.

Cecily.

I think your frankness does you great credit, Ernest. If you will allow me, I will copy your remarks into my diary. (*Goes over to table and begins writing in diary.*)

Algernon.
Do you really keep a diary? I'd give anything to look at it. May I?

Cecily.
Oh no. (*Puts her hand over it.*) You see, it is simply a very young girl's record of her own thoughts and impressions, and consequently meant for publication. When it appears in volume form I hope you will order a copy. But pray, Ernest, don't stop. I delight in taking down from dictation. I have reached 'absolute perfection.' You can go on. I am quite ready for more.

Algernon.
(*Somewhat taken aback.*) Ahem! Ahem!

Cecily.
Oh, don't cough, Ernest. When one is dictating one should speak fluently and not cough. Besides, I don't know how to spell a cough. (*Writes as* ALGERNON *speaks.*)

Algernon.
(*Speaking very rapidly.*) Cecily, ever since I first looked upon your wonderful and incomparable beauty, I have dared to love you wildly, passionately, devotedly, hopelessly.

Cecily.
I don't think that you should tell me that you love me wildly, passionately, devotedly, hopelessly. Hopelessly doesn't seem to make much sense, does it?

Algernon.
Cecily.

(*Enter* MERRIMAN.)

Merriman.
The dog-cart is waiting, sir.

Algernon.
Tell it to come round next week, at the same hour.

Merriman.
(*Looks at* CECILY, *who makes no sign.*) Yes, sir.

(MERRIMAN *retires.*)

Cecily.
Uncle Jack would be very much annoyed if he knew you were staying on till next week, at the same hour.

Algernon.

Oh, I don't care about Jack. I don't care for anybody in the whole world but you. I love you, Cecily. You will marry me, won't you?

Cecily.

You silly boy! Of course. Why, we have been engaged for the last three months.

Algernon.

For the last three months?

Cecily.

Yes, it will be exactly three months on Thursday.

Algernon.

But how did we become engaged?

Cecily.

Well, ever since dear Uncle Jack first confessed to us that he had a younger brother who was very wicked and bad, you of course have formed the chief topic of conversation between myself and Miss Prism. And of course a man who is much talked about is always very attractive. One feels there must be something in him, after all. I daresay it was foolish of me, but I fell in love with you, Ernest.

Algernon.

Darling. And when was the engagement actually settled?

Cecily.

On the 14th of February last. Worn out by your entire ignorance of my existence, I determined to end the matter one way or the other, and after a long struggle with myself I accepted you under this dear old tree here. The next day I bought this little ring in your name, and this is the little bangle with the true lover's knot I promised you always to wear.

Algernon.

Did I give you this? It's very pretty, isn't it?

Cecily.

Yes, you've wonderfully good taste, Ernest. It's the excuse I've always given for your leading such a bad life. And this is the box in which I keep all your dear letters. (*Kneels at table, opens box, and produces letters tied up with blue ribbon.*)

Algernon.
My letters! But, my own sweet Cecily, I have never written you any letters.

Cecily.
You need hardly remind me of that, Ernest. I remember only too well that I was forced to write your letters for you. I wrote always three times a week, and sometimes oftener.

Algernon.
Oh, do let me read them, Cecily?

Cecily.
Oh, I couldn't possibly. They would make you far too conceited. (*Replaces box.*) The three you wrote me after I had broken off the engagement are so beautiful, and so badly spelled, that even now I can hardly read them without crying a little.

Algernon.
But was our engagement ever broken off?

Cecily.
Of course it was. On the 22nd of last March. You can see the entry if you like. (*Shows diary.*) 'Today I broke off my engagement with Ernest. I feel it is better to do so. The weather still continues charming.'

Algernon.
But why on earth did you break it off? What had I done? I had done nothing at all. Cecily, I am very much hurt indeed to hear you broke it off. Particularly when the weather was so charming.

Cecily.
It would hardly have been a really serious engagement if it hadn't been broken off at least once. But I forgave you before the week was out.

Algernon.
(*Crossing to her, and kneeling.*) What a perfect angel you are, Cecily.

Cecily.
You dear romantic boy. (*He kisses her, she puts her fingers through his hair.*) I hope your hair curls naturally, does it?

Algernon.
Yes, darling, with a little help from others.

Cecily.
I am so glad.

Algernon.
You'll never break off our engagement again, Cecily?

Cecily.
I don't think I could break it off now that I have actually met you. Besides, of course, there is the question of your name.

Algernon.
Yes, of course. (*Nervously.*)

Cecily.
You must not laugh at me, darling, but it had always been a girlish dream of mine to love some one whose name was Ernest. (ALGERNON *rises,* CECILY *also.*) There is something in that name that seems to inspire absolute confidence. I pity any poor married woman whose husband is not called Ernest.

Algernon.
But, my dear child, do you mean to say you could not love me if I had some other name?

Cecily.
But what name?

Algernon.
Oh, any name you like—Algernon—for instance . . .

Cecily.
But I don't like the name of Algernon.

Algernon.
Well, my own dear, sweet, loving little darling, I really can't see why you should object to the name of Algernon. It is not at all a bad name. In fact, it is rather an aristocratic name. Half of the chaps who get into the Bankruptcy Court are called Algernon. But seriously, Cecily . . . (*Moving to her.*) if my name was Algy, couldn't you love me?

Cecily.
(*Rising.*) I might respect you, Ernest, I might admire your character, but I fear that I should not be able to give you my undivided attention.

Algernon.
Ahem! Cecily! (*Picking up hat.*) Your Rector here is, I suppose, thoroughly experienced in the practice of all the rites and ceremonials of the Church?

Cecily.
Oh, yes. Dr Chasuble is a most learned man. He has never written a single book, so you can imagine how much he knows.

Algernon.
I must see him at once on a most important christening—I mean on most important business.

Cecily.
Oh!

Algernon.
I shan't be away more than half an hour.

Cecily.
Considering that we have been engaged since February the 14th, and that I only met you to-day for the first time, I think it is rather hard that you should leave me for so long a period as half an hour. Couldn't you make it twenty minutes?

Algernon.
I'll be back in no time. (*Kisses her and rushes down the garden.*)

Cecily.
What an impetuous boy he is! I like his hair so much. I must enter his proposal in my diary.

(*Enter* MERRIMAN.)

Merriman.
A Miss Fairfax has just called to see Mr Worthing. On very important business, Miss Fairfax states.

Cecily.
Isn't Mr Worthing in his library?

Merriman.
Mr Worthing went over in the direction of the Rectory some time ago.

Cecily.
Pray ask the lady to come out here; Mr Worthing is sure to be back soon. And you can bring tea.

Merriman.
Yes, Miss.

(*Goes out.*)

Cecily.
Miss Fairfax! I suppose one of the many good elderly women who are associated with Uncle Jack in some of his philanthropic work in London. I don't quite

like women who are interested in philanthropic work.
I think it is so forward of them.

(*Enter* MERRIMAN.)

Merriman.
Miss Fairfax.

(*Enter* GWENDOLEN. *Exit* MERRIMAN.)

Cecily.
(*Advancing to meet her.*) Pray let me introduce myself to you. My name is Cecily Cardew.

Gwendolen.
Cecily Cardew? (*Moving to her and shaking hands.*)
What a very sweet name! Something tells me that
we are going to be great friends. I like you already
more than I can say. My first impressions of people
are never wrong.

Cecily.
How nice of you to like me so much after we have
known each other such a comparatively short time.
Pray sit down.

Gwendolen.
(*Still standing up.*) I may call you Cecily, may I not?

Cecily.
With pleasure!

Gwendolen.
And you will always call me Gwendolen, won't you?

Cecily.
If you wish.

Gwendolen.
Then that is all quite settled, is it not?

Cecily.
I hope so. (*A pause. They both sit down together.*)

Gwendolen.
Perhaps this might be a favourable opportunity for
my mentioning who I am. My father is Lord Bracknell. You have never heard of papa, I suppose?

Cecily.
I don't think so.

Gwendolen.
Outside the family circle, papa, I am glad to say, is
entirely unknown. I think that is quite as it should
be. The home seems to me to be the proper sphere

for the man. And certainly once a man begins to neglect his domestic duties he becomes painfully effeminate, does he not? And I don't like that. It makes men so very attractive. Cecily, mamma, whose views on education are remarkably strict, has brought me up to be extremely short-sighted; it is part of her system; so do you mind my looking at you through my glasses?

Cecily.

Oh! not at all, Gwendolen. I am very fond of being looked at.

Gwendolen.

(*After examining* CECILY *carefully through a lorgnette.*) You are here on a short visit, I suppose.

Cecily.

Oh no! I live here.

Gwendolen.

(*Severely.*) Really? Your mother, no doubt, or some female relative of advanced years, resides here also?

Cecily.

Oh no! I have no mother, nor, in fact, any relations.

Gwendolen.

Indeed?

Cecily.

My dear guardian, with the assistance of Miss Prism, has the arduous task of looking after me.

Gwendolen.

Your guardian?

Cecily.

Yes, I am Mr Worthing's ward.

Gwendolen.

Oh! It is strange he never mentioned to me that he had a ward. How secretive of him! He grows more interesting hourly. I am not sure, however, that the news inspires me with feelings of unmixed delight. (*Rising and going to her.*) I am very fond of you, Cecily; I have liked you ever since I met you! But I am bound to state that now that I know that you are Mr Worthing's ward, I cannot help expressing a wish you were—well, just a little older than you seem to be—and not quite so very alluring in appearance. In fact, if I may speak candidly——

Cecily.

Pray do! I think that whenever one has anything unpleasant to say, one should always be quite candid.

Gwendolen.

Well, to speak with perfect candour, Cecily, I wish that you were fully forty-two, and more than usually plain for your age. Ernest has a strong upright nature. He is the very soul of truth and honour. Disloyalty would be as impossible to him as deception. But even men of the noblest possible moral character are extremely susceptible to the influence of the physical charms of others. Modern, no less than Ancient History, supplies us with many most painful examples of what I refer to. If it were not so, indeed, History would be quite unreadable.

Cecily.

I beg your pardon, Gwendolen, did you say Ernest?

Gwendolen.

Yes.

Cecily.

Oh, but it is not Mr Ernest Worthing who is my guardian. It is his brother—his elder brother.

Gwendolen.

(*Sitting down again.*) Ernest never mentioned to me that he had a brother.

Cecily.

I am sorry to say they have not been on good terms for a long time.

Gwendolen.

Ah! that accounts for it. And now that I think of it I have never heard any man mention his brother. The subject seems distasteful to most men. Cecily, you have lifted a load from my mind. I was growing almost anxious. It would have been terrible if any cloud had come across a friendship like ours, would it not? Of course you are quite, quite sure that it is not Mr Ernest Worthing who is your guardian?

Cecily.

Quite sure. (*A pause.*) In fact, I am going to be his.

Gwendolen.

(*Inquiringly.*) I beg your pardon?

Cecily.

(*Rather shy and confidingly.*) Dearest Gwendolen,

there is no reason why I should make a secret of it to you. Our little county newspaper is sure to chronicle the fact next week. Mr Ernest Worthing and I are engaged to be married.

Gwendolen.
(*Quite politely, rising.*) My darling Cecily, I think there must be some slight error. Mr Ernest Worthing is engaged to me. The announcement will appear in the *Morning Post* on Saturday at the latest.

Cecily.
(*Very politely, rising.*) I am afraid you must be under some misconception. Ernest proposed to me exactly ten minutes ago. (*Shows diary.*)

Gwendolen.
(*Examines diary through her lorgnette carefully.*) It is very curious, for he asked me to be his wife yesterday afternoon at 5.30. If you would care to verify the incident, pray do so. (*Produces diary of her own.*) I never travel without my diary. One should always have something sensational to read in the train. I am so sorry, dear Cecily, if it is any disappointment to you, but I am afraid I have the prior claim.

Cecily.
It would distress me more than I can tell you, dear Gwendolen, if it caused you any mental or physical anguish, but I feel bound to point out that since Ernest proposed to you he clearly has changed his mind.

Gwendolen.
(*Meditatively.*) If the poor fellow has been entrapped into any foolish promise, I shall consider it my duty to rescue him at once, and with a firm hand.

Cecily.
(*Thoughtfully and sadly.*) Whatever unfortunate entanglement my dear boy may have got into, I will never reproach him with it after we are married.

Gwendolen.
Do you allude to me, Miss Cardew, as an entanglement? You are presumptuous. On an occasion of this kind it becomes more than a moral duty to speak one's mind. It becomes a pleasure.

Cecily.
Do you suggest, Miss Fairfax, that I entrapped Er-

nest into an engagement? How dare you? This is no time for wearing the shallow mask of manners. When I see a spade I call it a spade.

Gwendolen.
(*Satirically.*) I am glad to say that I have never seen a spade. It is obvious that our social spheres have been widely different.

(*Enter* MERRIMAN, *followed by the footman. He carries a salver, table cloth, and plate stand.* CECILY *is about to retort. The presence of the servants exercises a restraining influence, under which both girls chafe.*)

Merriman.
Shall I lay tea here as usual, Miss?

Cecily.
(*Sternly, in a calm voice.*) Yes, as usual. (MERRIMAN *begins to clear table and lay cloth. A long pause.* CECILY *and* GWENDOLEN *glare at each other.*)

Gwendolen.
Are there many interesting walks in the vicinity, Miss Cardew?

Cecily.
Oh! yes! a great many. From the top of one of the hills quite close one can see five counties.

Gwendolen.
Five counties! I don't think I should like that; I hate crowds.

Cecily.
(*Sweetly.*) I suppose that is why you live in town? (GWENDOLEN *bites her lip, and beats her foot nervously with her parasol.*)

Gwendolen.
(*Looking around.*) Quite a well-kept garden this is, Miss Cardew.

Cecily.
So glad you like it, Miss Fairfax.

Gwendolen.
I had no idea there were any flowers in the country.

Cecily.
Oh, flowers are as common here, Miss Fairfax, as people are in London.

Gwendolen.
Personally I cannot understand how anybody manages to exist in the country, if anybody who is anybody does. The country always bores me to death.

Cecily.
Ah! This is what the newspapers call agricultural depression, is it not? I believe the aristocracy are suffering very much from it just at present. It is almost an epidemic amongst them, I have been told. May I offer you some tea, Miss Fairfax?

Gwendolen.
(*With elaborate politeness.*) Thank you. (*Aside.*) Detestable girl! But I require tea!

Cecily.
(*Sweetly.*) Sugar?

Gwendolen.
(*Superciliously.*) No, thank you. Sugar is not fashionable any more. (CECILY *looks angrily at her, takes up the tongs and puts four lumps of sugar into the cup.*)

Cecily.
(*Severely.*) Cake or bread and butter?

Gwendolen.
(*In a bored manner.*) Bread and butter, please. Cake is rarely seen at the best houses nowadays.

Cecily.
(*Cuts a very large slice of cake and puts it on the tray.*) Hand that to Miss Fairfax.

(MERRIMAN *does so, and goes out with footman.* GWENDOLEN *drinks the tea and makes a grimace. Puts down cup at once, reaches out her hand to the bread and butter, looks at it, and finds it is cake. Rises in indignation.*)

Gwendolen.
You have filled my tea with lumps of sugar, and though I asked most distinctly for bread and butter, you have given me cake. I am known for the gentleness of my disposition, and the extraordinary sweetness of my nature, but I warn you, Miss Cardew, you may go too far.

Cecily.
(*Rising.*) To save my poor, innocent, trusting boy

from the machinations of any other girl there are no lengths to which I would not go.

Gwendolen.

From the moment I saw you I distrusted you. I felt that you were false and deceitful. I am never deceived in such matters. My first impressions of people are invariably right.

Cecily.

It seems to me, Miss Fairfax, that I am trespassing on your valuable time. No doubt you have many other calls of a similar character to make in the neighbourhood.

(*Enter* JACK.)

Gwendolen.

(*Catching sight of him.*) Ernest! My own Ernest!

Jack.

Gwendolen! Darling! (*Offers to kiss her.*)

Gwendolen.

(*Drawing back.*) A moment! May I ask if you are engaged to be married to this young lady? (*Points to* CECILY.)

Jack.

(*Laughing.*) To dear little Cecily! Of course not! What could have put such an idea into your pretty little head?

Gwendolen.

Thank you. You may! (*Offers her cheek.*)

Cecily.

(*Very sweetly.*) I knew there must be some misunderstanding, Miss Fairfax. The gentleman whose arm is at present round your waist is my guardian, Mr John Worthing.

Gwendolen.

I beg your pardon?

Cecily.

This is Uncle Jack.

Gwendolen.

(*Receding.*) Jack! Oh!

(*Enter* ALGERNON.)

Cecily.

Here is Ernest.

Algernon.
(*Goes straight over to* CECILY *without noticing anyone else.*) My own love! (*Offers to kiss her.*)

Cecily.
(*Drawing back.*) A moment, Ernest! May I ask you —are you engaged to be married to this young lady?

Algernon.
(*Looking round.*) To what young lady? Good heavens! Gwendolen!

Cecily.
Yes: to good heavens, Gwendolen, I mean to Gwendolen.

Algernon.
(*Laughing.*) Of course not! What could have put such an idea into your pretty little head?

Cecily.
Thank you. (*Presenting her cheek to be kissed.*) You may. (ALGERNON *kisses her.*)

Gwendolen.
I felt there was some slight error, Miss Cardew. The gentleman who is now embracing you is my cousin, Mr Algernon Moncrieff.

Cecily.
(*Breaking away from* ALGERNON.) Algernon Moncrieff! Oh! (*The two girls move towards each other and put their arms round each other's waists as if for protection.*)

Cecily.
Are you called Algernon?

Algernon.
I cannot deny it.

Cecily.
Oh!

Gwendolen.
Is your name really John?

Jack.
(*Standing rather proudly.*) I could deny it if I liked. I could deny anything if I liked. But my name certainly is John. It has been John for years.

Cecily.
(*To* GWENDOLEN.) A gross deception has been practised on both of us.

Gwendolen.
My poor wounded Cecily!

Cecily.

My sweet wronged Gwendolen!

Gwendolen.

(*Slowly and seriously.*) You will call me sister, will you not? (*They embrace.* JACK *and* ALGERNON *groan and walk up and down.*)

Cecily.

(*Rather brightly.*) There is just one question I would like to be allowed to ask my guardian.

Gwendolen.

An admirable idea! Mr Worthing, there is just one question I would like to be permitted to put to you. Where is your brother Ernest? We are both engaged to be married to your brother Ernest, so it is a matter of some importance to us to know where your brother Ernest is at present.

Jack.

(*Slowly and hesitatingly.*) Gwendolen—Cecily—it is very painful for me to be forced to speak the truth. It is the first time in my life that I have ever been reduced to such a painful position, and I am really quite inexperienced in doing anything of the kind. However, I will tell you quite frankly that I have no brother Ernest. I have no brother at all. I never had a brother in my life, and I certainly have not the smallest intention of ever having one in the future.

Cecily.

(*Surprised.*) No brother at all?

Jack.

(*Cheerily.*) None!

Gwendolen.

(*Severely.*) Had you never a brother of any kind?

Jack.

(*Pleasantly.*) Never. Not even of any kind.

Gwendolen.

I am afraid it is quite clear, Cecily, that neither of us is engaged to be married to anyone.

Cecily.

It is not a very pleasant position for a young girl suddenly to find herself in. Is it?

Gwendolen.

Let us go into the house. They will hardly venture to come after us there.

Cecily.
No, men are so cowardly, aren't they?

(*They retire into the house with scornful looks.*)

Jack.
This ghastly state of things is what you call Bunbury-ing I suppose?

Algernon.
Yes, and a perfectly wonderful Bunbury it is. The most wonderful Bunbury I have ever had in my life.

Jack.
Well, you've no right whatsoever to Bunbury here.

Algernon.
That is absurd. One has a right to Bunbury any-where one chooses. Every serious Bunburyist knows that.

Jack.
Serious Bunburyist? Good heavens!

Algernon.
Well, one must be serious about something, if one wants to have any amusement in life. I happen to be serious about Bunburying. What on earth you are serious about I haven't got the remotest idea. About everything, I should fancy. You have such an ab-solutely trivial nature.

Jack.
Well, the only small satisfaction I have in the whole of this wretched business is that your friend Bunbury is quite exploded. You won't be able to run down to the country quite so often as you used to do, dear Algy. And a very good thing too.

Algernon.
Your brother is a little off colour, isn't he, dear Jack? You won't be able to disappear to London quite so frequently as your wicked custom was. And not a bad thing either.

Jack.
As for your conduct towards Miss Cardew, I must say that your taking in a sweet, simple, innocent girl like that is quite inexcusable. To say nothing of the fact that she is my ward.

Algernon.
I can see no possible defence at all for your deceiv-

ing a brilliant, clever, thoroughly experienced young
lady like Miss Fairfax. To say nothing of the fact
that she is my cousin.

Jack.
I wanted to be engaged to Gwendolen, that is all, I
love her.

Algernon.
Well, I simply wanted to be engaged to Cecily. I adore
her.

Jack.
There is certainly no chance of your marrying Miss
Cardew.

Algernon.
I don't think there is much likelihood, Jack, of you
and Miss Fairfax being united.

Jack.
Well, that is no business of yours.

Algernon.
If it was my business, I wouldn't talk about it. (*Begins to eat muffins.*) It is very vulgar to talk about
one's business. Only people like stockbrokers do that,
and then merely at dinner parties.

Jack.
How you can sit there, calmly eating muffins when
we are in this horrible trouble, I can't make out. You
seem to me to be perfectly heartless.

Algernon.
Well, I can't eat muffins in an agitated manner. The
butter would probably get on my cuffs. One should
always eat muffins quite calmly. It is the only way
to eat them.

Jack.
I say it's perfectly heartless your eating muffins at
all, under the circumstances.

Algernon.
When I am in trouble, eating is the only thing that
consoles me. Indeed, when I am in really great trouble, as any one who knows me intimately will tell
you, I refuse everything except food and drink. At
the present moment I am eating muffins because I
am unhappy. Besides, I am particularly fond of muffins. (*Rising.*)

Jack.
(*Rising.*) Well, there is no reason why you should eat them all in that greedy way. (*Takes muffins from* ALGERNON.)

Algernon.
(*Offering tea-cake.*) I wish you would have tea-cake instead. I don't like tea-cake.

Jack.
Good heavens! I suppose a man may eat his own muffins in his own garden.

Algernon.
But you have just said it was perfectly heartless to eat muffins.

Jack.
I said it was perfectly heartless of you, under the circumstances. That is a very different thing.

Algernon.
That may be. But the muffins are the same. (*He seizes the muffin-dish from* JACK.)

Jack.
Algy, I wish to goodness you would go.

Algernon.
You can't possibly ask me to go without having some dinner. It's absurd. I never go without my dinner. No one ever does, except vegetarians and people like that. Besides I have just made arrangements with Dr Chasuble to be christened at a quarter to six under the name of Ernest.

Jack.
My dear fellow, the sooner you give up that nonsense the better. I made arrangements this morning with Dr Chasuble to be christened myself at 5.30, and I naturally will take the name of Ernest. Gwendolen would wish it. We can't both be christened Ernest. It's absurd. Besides, I have a perfect right to be christened if I like. There is no evidence at all that I have ever been christened by anybody. I should think it extremely probable I never was, and so does Dr Chasuble. It is entirely different in your case. You have been christened already.

Algernon.
Yes, but I have not been christened for years.

Jack.

Yes, but you have been christened. That is the important thing.

Algernon.

Quite so. So I know my constitution can stand it. If you are not quite sure about your ever having been christened, I must say I think it rather dangerous your venturing on it now. It might make you very unwell. You can hardly have forgotten that someone very closely connected with you was very nearly carried off this week in Paris by a severe chill.

Jack.

Yes, but you said yourself that a severe chill was not hereditary.

Algernon.

It usen't to be, I know——but I daresay it is now. Science is always making wonderful improvements in things.

Jack.

(*Picking up the muffin-dish.*) Oh, that is nonsense; you are always talking nonsense.

Algernon.

Jack, you are at the muffins again! I wish you wouldn't. There are only two left. (*Takes them.*) I told you I was particularly fond of muffins.

Jack.

But I hate tea-cake.

Algernon.

Why on earth then do you allow tea-cake to be served up for your guests? What ideas you have of hospitality!

Jack.

Algernon! I have already told you to go. I don't want you here. Why don't you go!

Algernon.

I haven't quite finished my tea yet! and there is still one muffin left. (*JACK groans, and sinks into a chair. ALGERNON continues eating.*)

ACT DROP

THIRD ACT

SCENE

Drawing-room at the Manor House

(GWENDOLEN *and* CECILY *are at the window, looking out into the garden.*)

Gwendolen.
The fact that they did not follow us at once into the house, as anyone else would have done, seems to me to show that they have some sense of shame left.

Cecily.
They have been eating muffins. That looks like repentance.

Gwendolen.
(*After a pause.*) They don't seem to notice us at all. Couldn't you cough?

Cecily.
But I haven't got a cough.

Gwendolen.
They're looking at us. What effrontery!

Cecily.
They're approaching. That's very forward of them.

Gwendolen.
Let us preserve a dignified silence.

Cecily.
Certainly. It's the only thing to do now.

(*Enter* JACK *followed by* ALGERNON. *They whistle some dreadful popular air from a British Opera.*)

Gwendolen.
This dignified silence seems to produce an unpleasant effect.

Cecily.
A most distasteful one.

Gwendolen.
But we will not be the first to speak.

Cecily.
Certainly not.

Gwendolen.
Mr Worthing, I have something very particular to ask you. Much depends on your reply.

Cecily.
Gwendolen, your common sense is invaluable. Mr Moncrieff, kindly answer me the following question. Why did you pretend to be my guardian's brother?

Algernon.
In order that I might have an opportunity of meeting you.

Cecily.
(*To* GWENDOLEN.) That certainly seems a satisfactory explanation, does it not?

Gwendolen.
Yes, dear, if you can believe him.

Cecily.
I don't. But that does not affect the wonderful beauty of his answer.

Gwendolen.
True. In matters of grave importance, style, not sincerity, is the vital thing. Mr Worthing, what explanation can you offer to me for pretending to have a brother? Was it in order that you might have an opportunity of coming up to town to see me as often as possible?

Jack.
Can you doubt it, Miss Fairfax?

Gwendolen.
I have the gravest doubts upon the subject. But I intend to crush them. This is not the moment for German scepticism. (*Moving to* CECILY.) Their explanations appear to be quite satisfactory, especially Mr Worthing's. That seems to me to have the stamp of truth upon it.

Cecily.
I am more than content with what Mr Moncrieff said. His voice alone inspires one with absolute credulity.

Gwendolen.
Then you think we should forgive them?

Cecily.
Yes. I mean no.

Gwendolen.
True! I had forgotten. There are principles at stake that one cannot surrender. Which of us should tell them? The task is not a pleasant one.

Cecily.
Could we not both speak at the same time?

Gwendolen.
An excellent idea! I nearly always speak at the same time as other people. Will you take the time from me?

Cecily.
Certainly. (GWENDOLEN *beats time with uplifted finger.*)

Gwendolen and Cecily.
(*Speaking together.*) Your Christian names are still an insuperable barrier. That is all!

Jack and Algernon.
(*Speaking together.*) Our Christian names! Is that all? But we are going to be christened this afternoon.

Gwendolen.
(*To* JACK.) For my sake you are prepared to do this terrible thing?

Jack.
I am.

Cecily.
(*To* ALGERNON.) To please me you are ready to face this fearful ordeal?

Algernon.
I am!

Gwendolen.
How absurd to talk of the equality of the sexes! Where questions of self-sacrifice are concerned, men are infinitely beyond us.

Jack.
We are. (*Clasps hands with* ALGERNON.)

Cecily.
They have moments of physical courage of which we women know absolutely nothing.

Gwendolen.
(*To* JACK.) Darling!

Algernon.
(*To* CECILY.) Darling! (*They fall into each other's arms.*)

(*Enter* MERRIMAN. *When he enters he coughs loudly, seeing the situation.*)

Merriman.
Ahem! Ahem! Lady Bracknell.

Jack.
Good heavens!

(*Enter* LADY BRACKNELL. *The couples separate in alarm. Exit* MERRIMAN.)

Lady Bracknell.
Gwendolen! What does this mean?

Gwendolen.
Merely that I am engaged to be married to Mr Worthing, mamma.

Lady Bracknell.
Come here. Sit down. Sit down immediately. Hesitation of any kind is a sign of mental decay in the young, of physical weakness in the old. (*Turns to* JACK.) Apprised, sir, of my daughter's sudden flight by her trusty maid, whose confidence I purchased by means of a small coin, I followed her at once by a luggage train. Her unhappy father is, I am glad to say, under the impression that she is attending a more than usually lengthy lecture by the University Extension Scheme on the Influence of a Permanent Income on Thought. I do not propose to undeceive him. Indeed I have never undeceived him on any question. I would consider it wrong. But of course, you will clearly understand that all communication between yourself and my daughter must cease immediately from this moment. On this point, as indeed on all points, I am firm.

Jack.
I am engaged to be married to Gwendolen, Lady Bracknell!

Lady Bracknell.
You are nothing of the kind, sir. And now as regards Algernon! . . . Algernon!

Algernon.
Yes, Aunt Augusta.

Lady Bracknell.
May I ask if it is in this house that your invalid friend Mr Bunbury resides?

Algernon.
(*Stammering.*) Oh! No! Bunbury doesn't live here. Bunbury is somewhere else at present. In fact, Bunbury is dead.

Lady Bracknell.
Dead! When did Mr Bunbury die? His death must have been extremely sudden.

Algernon.
(*Airily.*) Oh! I killed Bunbury this afternoon. I mean poor Bunbury died this afternoon.

Lady Bracknell.
What did he die of?

Algernon.
Bunbury? Oh, he was quite exploded.

Lady Bracknell.
Exploded! Was he the victim of a revolutionary outrage? I was not aware that Mr Bunbury was interested in social legislation. If so, he is well punished for his morbidity.

Algernon.
My dear Aunt Augusta, I mean he was found out! The doctors found out that Bunbury could not live, that is what I mean—so Bunbury died.

Lady Bracknell.
He seems to have had great confidence in the opinion of his physicians. I am glad, however, that he made up his mind at the last to some definite course of action, and acted under proper medical advice. And now that we have finally got rid of this Mr Bunbury, may I ask, Mr Worthing, who is that young person whose hand my nephew Algernon is now holding in what seems to me a peculiarly unnecessary manner?

Jack.

That lady is Miss Cecily Cardew, my ward. (LADY BRACKNELL *bows coldly to* CECILY.)

Algernon.

I am engaged to be married to Cecily, Aunt Augusta.

Lady Bracknell.

I beg your pardon?

Cecily.

Mr Moncrieff and I are engaged to be married, Lady Bracknell.

Lady Bracknell.

(*With a shiver, crossing to the sofa and sitting down.*) I do not know whether there is anything peculiarly exciting in the air of this particular part of Hertford-shire, but the number of engagements that go on seems to me considerably above the proper average that statistics have laid down for our guidance. I think some preliminary inquiry on my part would not be out of place. Mr Worthing, is Miss Cardew at all connected with any of the larger railway stations in London? I merely desire information. Until yes-terday I had no idea that there were any families or persons whose origin was a Terminus. (JACK *looks perfectly furious, but restrains himself.*)

Jack.

(*In a cold, clear voice.*) Miss Cardew is the grand-daughter of the late Mr Thomas Cardew of 149 Bel-grave Square, S.W.; Gervase Park, Dorking, Surrey; and the Sporran, Fifeshire, N.B.

Lady Bracknell.

That sounds not unsatisfactory. Three addresses al-ways inspire confidence, even in tradesmen. But what proof have I of their authenticity?

Jack.

I have carefully preserved the Court Guides of the period. They are open to your inspection, Lady Brack-nell.

Lady Bracknell.

(*Grimly.*) I have known strange errors in that publi-cation.

Jack.

Miss Cardew's family solicitors are Messrs Markby, Markby, and Markby.

Lady Bracknell.
Markby, Markby, and Markby? A firm of the very highest position in their profession. Indeed I am told that one of the Mr Markby's is occasionally to be seen at dinner parties. So far I am satisfied.

Jack.
(*Very irritably.*) How extremely kind of you, Lady Bracknell! I have also in my possession, you will be pleased to hear, certificates of Miss Cardew's birth, baptism, whooping cough, registration, vaccination, confirmation, and the measles; both the German and the English variety.

Lady Bracknell.
Ah! A life crowded with incident, I see; though perhaps somewhat too exciting for a young girl. I am not myself in favour of premature experiences. (*Rises, looks at her watch.*) Gwendolen! the time approaches for our departure. We have not a moment to lose. As a matter of form, Mr Worthing, I had better ask you if Miss Cardew has any little fortune?

Jack.
Oh! about a hundred and thirty thousand pounds in the Funds. That is all. Good-bye, Lady Bracknell. So pleased to have seen you.

Lady Bracknell.
(*Sitting down again.*) A moment, Mr Worthing. A hundred and thirty thousand pounds! And in the Funds! Miss Cardew seems to me a most attractive young lady, now that I look at her. Few girls of the present day have any really solid qualities, any of the qualities that last, and improve with time. We live, I regret to say, in an age of surfaces. (*To* CECILY.) Come over here, dear. (CECILY *goes across.*) Pretty child! your dress is sadly simple, and your hair seems almost as Nature might have left it. But we can soon alter all that. A thoroughly experienced French maid produces a really marvellous result in a very brief space of time. I remember recommending one to young Lady Lancing, and after three months her own husband did not know her.

Jack.
And after six months nobody knew her.

Lady Bracknell.
(*Glares at* JACK *for a few moments. Then bends, with a practised smile, to* CECILY.) Kindly turn round, sweet child. (CECILY *turns completely round.*) No, the side view is what I want. (CECILY *presents her profile.*) Yes, quite as I expected. There are distinct social possibilities in your profile. The two weak points in our age are its want of principle and its want of profile. The chin a little higher, dear. Style largely depends on the way the chin is worn. They are worn very high, just at present, Algernon!

Algernon.
Yes, Aunt Augusta!

Lady Bracknell.
There are distinct social possibilities in Miss Cardew's profile.

Algernon.
Cecily is the sweetest, dearest, prettiest girl in the whole world. And I don't care twopence about social possibilities.

Lady Bracknell.
Never speak disrespectfully of Society, Algernon. Only people who can't get into it do that. (*To* CECILY.) Dear child, of course you know that Algernon has nothing but his debts to depend upon. But I do not approve of mercenary marriages. When I married Lord Bracknell I had no fortune of any kind. But I never dreamed for a moment of allowing that to stand in my way. Well, I suppose I must give my consent.

Algernon.
Thank you, Aunt Augusta.

Lady Bracknell.
Cecily, you may kiss me!

Cecily.
(*Kisses her.*) Thank you, Lady Bracknell.

Lady Bracknell.
You may also address me as Aunt Augusta for the future.

Cecily.
Thank you, Aunt Augusta.

Lady Bracknell.
The marriage, I think, had better take place quite soon.

Algernon.
Thank you, Aunt Augusta.

Cecily.
Thank you, Aunt Augusta.

Lady Bracknell.
To speak frankly, I am not in favour of long engagements. They give people the opportunity of finding out each other's character before marriage, which I think is never advisable.

Jack.
I beg your pardon for interrupting you, Lady Bracknell, but this engagement is quite out of the question. I am Miss Cardew's guardian, and she cannot marry without my consent until she comes of age. That consent I absolutely decline to give.

Lady Bracknell.
Upon what grounds, may I ask? Algernon is an extremely, I may almost say an ostentatiously, eligible young man. He has nothing, but he looks everything. What more can one desire?

Jack.
It pains me very much to have to speak frankly to you, Lady Bracknell, about your nephew, but the fact is that I do not approve at all of his moral character. I suspect him of being untruthful. (ALGERNON *and* CECILY *look at him in indignant amazement.*)

Lady Bracknell.
Untruthful! My nephew Algernon? Impossible! He is an Oxonian.

Jack.
I fear there can be no possible doubt about the matter. This afternoon during my temporary absence in London on an important question of romance, he obtained admission to my house by means of the false pretence of being my brother. Under an assumed name he drank, I've just been informed by my butler, an entire pint bottle of my Perrier-Jouet, Brut, '89; wine I was specially reserving for myself.

Continuing his disgraceful deception, he succeeded in the course of the afternoon in alienating the affections of my only ward. He subsequently stayed to tea, and devoured every single muffin. And what makes his conduct all the more heartless is, that he was perfectly well aware from the first that I have no brother, that I never had a brother, and that I don't intend to have a brother, not even of any kind. I distinctly told him so myself yesterday afternoon.

Lady Bracknell.

Ahem! Mr Worthing, after careful consideration I have decided entirely to overlook my nephew's conduct to you.

Jack.

That is very generous of you, Lady Bracknell. My own decision, however, is unalterable. I decline to give my consent.

Lady Bracknell.

(*To* CECILY.) Come here, sweet child. (CECILY *goes over*.) How old are you, dear?

Cecily.

Well, I am really only eighteen, but I always admit to twenty when I go to evening parties.

Lady Bracknell.

You are perfectly right in making some slight alteration. Indeed, no woman should ever be quite accurate about her age. It looks so calculating. . . . (*In a meditative manner.*) Eighteen, but admitting to twenty at evening parties. Well, it will not be very long before you are of age and free from the restraints of tutelage. So I don't think your guardian's consent is, after all, a matter of any importance.

Jack.

Pray excuse me, Lady Bracknell, for interrupting you again, but it is only fair to tell you that according to the terms of her grandfather's will Miss Cardew does not come legally of age till she is thirty-five.

Lady Bracknell.

That does not seem to me to be a grave objection. Thirty-five is a very attractive age. London society is full of women of the very highest birth who have, of their own free choice, remained thirty-five for years. Lady Dumbleton is an instance in point. To my own knowledge she has been thirty-five ever since she arrived at the age of forty, which was many years ago now. I see no reason why our dear Cecily should not be even still more attractive at the age you mention than she is at present. There will be a large accumulation of property.

Cecily.
Algy, could you wait for me till I was thirty-five?

Algernon.
Of course I could, Cecily. You know I could.

Cecily.
Yes, I felt it instinctively, but I couldn't wait all that time. I hate waiting even five minutes for anybody. It always makes me rather cross. I am not punctual myself, I know, but I do like punctuality in others, and waiting, even to be married, is quite out of the question.

Algernon.
Then what is to be done, Cecily?

Cecily.
I don't know, Mr Moncrieff.

Lady Bracknell.
My dear Mr Worthing, as Miss Cardew states positively that she cannot wait till she is thirty-five—a remark which I am bound to say seems to me to show a somewhat impatient nature—I would beg of you to reconsider your decision.

Jack.
But my dear Lady Bracknell, the matter is entirely in your own hands. The moment you consent to my marriage with Gwendolen, I will most gladly allow your nephew to form an alliance with my ward.

Lady Bracknell.
(*Rising and drawing herself up.*) You must be quite aware that what you propose is out of the question.

Jack.
Then a passionate celibacy is all that any of us can look forward to.

Lady Bracknell.
That is not the destiny I propose for Gwendolen. Algernon, of course, can choose for himself. (*Pulls out her watch.*) Come, dear (GWENDOLEN *rises.*),

we have already missed five, if not six, trains. To miss any more might expose us to comment on the platform.

(*Enter* DR CHASUBLE.)

Chasuble.
Everything is quite ready for the christenings.

Lady Bracknell.
The christenings, sir! Is not that somewhat premature?

Chasuble.
(*Looking rather puzzled, and pointing to* JACK *and* ALGERNON.) Both these gentlemen have expressed a desire for immediate baptism.

Lady Bracknell.
At their age? The idea is grotesque and irreligious! Algernon, I forbid you to be baptized. I will not hear of such excesses. Lord Bracknell would be highly displeased if he learned that that was the way in which you wasted your time and money.

Chasuble.
Am I to understand then that there are to be no christenings at all this afternoon?

Jack.
I don't think that, as things are now, it would be of much practical value to either of us, Dr Chasuble.

Chasuble.
I am grieved to hear such sentiments from you, Mr Worthing. They savour of the heretical views of the Anabaptists, views that I have completely refuted in four of my unpublished sermons. However, as your present mood seems to be one peculiarly secular, I will return to the church at once. Indeed, I have just been informed by the pew-opener that for the last hour and a half Miss Prism has been waiting for me in the vestry.

Lady Bracknell.
(*Starting.*) Miss Prism! Did I hear you mention a Miss Prism?

Chasuble.
Yes, Lady Bracknell. I am on my way to join her.

Lady Bracknell.
Pray allow me to detain you for a moment. This

matter may prove to be one of vital importance to Lord Bracknell and myself. Is this Miss Prism a female of repellent aspect, remotely connected with education?

Chasuble.
(*Somewhat indignantly.*) She is the most cultivated of ladies, and the very picture of respectability.

Lady Bracknell.
It is obviously the same person. May I ask what position she holds in your household?

Chasuble.
(*Severely.*) I am a celibate, madam.

Jack.
(*Interposing.*) Miss Prism, Lady Bracknell, has been for the last three years Miss Cardew's esteemed governess and valued companion.

Lady Bracknell.
In spite of what I hear of her, I must see her at once. Let her be sent for.

Chasuble.
(*Looking off.*) She approaches; she is nigh.

(*Enter* MISS PRISM *hurriedly.*)

Miss Prism.
I was told you expected me in the vestry, dear Canon. I have been waiting for you there for an hour and three-quarters. (*Catches sight of* LADY BRACKNELL, *who has fixed her with a stony glare.* MISS PRISM *grows pale and quails. She looks anxiously round as if desirous to escape.*)

Lady Bracknell.
(*In a severe, judicial voice.*) Prism! (MISS PRISM *bows her head in shame.*) Come here, Prism! (MISS PRISM *approaches in a humble manner.*) Prism! Where is that baby? (*General consternation. The Canon starts back in horror.* ALGERNON *and* JACK *pretend to be anxious to shield* CECILY *and* GWENDOLEN *from hearing the details of a terrible public scandal.*) Twenty-eight years ago, Prism, you left Lord Bracknell's house, Number 104, Upper Grosvenor Street, in charge of a perambulator that contained a baby of the male sex. You never returned.

A few weeks later, through the elaborate investigations of the Metropolitan police, the perambulator was discovered at midnight standing by itself in a remote corner of Bayswater. It contained the manuscript of a three-volume novel of more than usually revolting sentimentality. (MISS PRISM *starts in involuntary indignation.*) But the baby was not there. (*Every one looks at* MISS PRISM.) Prism! Where is that baby? (*A pause.*)

Miss Prism.

Lady Bracknell, I admit with shame that I do not know. I only wish I did. The plain facts of the case are these. On the morning of the day you mention, a day that is for ever branded on my memory, I prepared as usual to take the baby out in its perambulator. I had also with me a somewhat old, but capacious hand-bag in which I had intended to place the manuscript of a work of fiction that I had written during my few unoccupied hours. In a moment of mental abstraction, for which I can never forgive myself, I deposited the manuscript in the bassinette and placed the baby in the hand-bag.

Jack.

(*Who has been listening attentively.*) But where did you deposit the hand-bag?

Miss Prism.

Do not ask me, Mr Worthing.

Jack.

Miss Prism, this is a matter of no small importance to me. I insist on knowing where you deposited the hand-bag that contained that infant.

Miss Prism.

I left it in the cloak-room of one of the larger railway stations in London.

Jack.

What railway station?

Miss Prism.

(*Quite crushed.*) Victoria. The Brighton line. (*Sinks into a chair.*)

Jack.

I must retire to my room for a moment. Gwendolen, wait here for me.

Gwendolen.
If you are not too long, I will wait here for you all my life. (*Exit* JACK *in great excitement.*)

Chasuble.
What do you think this means, Lady Bracknell?

Lady Bracknell.
I dare not even suspect, Dr Chasuble. I need hardly tell you that in families of high position strange coincidences are not supposed to occur. They are hardly considered the thing.

(*Noises heard overhead as if some one was throwing trunks about. Every one looks up.*)

Cecily.
Uncle Jack seems strangely agitated.

Chasuble.
Your guardian has a very emotional nature.

Lady Bracknell.
This noise is extremely unpleasant. It sounds as if he was having an argument. I dislike arguments of any kind. They are always vulgar, and often convincing.

Chasuble.
(*Looking up.*) It has stopped now. (*The noise is redoubled.*)

Lady Bracknell.
I wish he would arrive at some conclusion.

Gwendolen.
This suspense is terrible. I hope it will last.

(*Enter* JACK *with a hand-bag of black leather in his hand.*)

Jack.
(*Rushing over to* MISS PRISM.) Is this the handbag, Miss Prism? Examine it carefully before you speak. The happiness of more than one life depends on your answer.

Miss Prism.
(*Calmly.*) It seems to be mine. Yes, here is the injury it received through the upsetting of a Gower Street omnibus in younger and happier days. Here is the stain on the lining caused by the explosion of a temperance beverage, an incident that occurred at

Leamington. And here, on the lock, are my initials.
I had forgotten that in an extravagant mood I had
had them placed there. The bag is undoubtedly mine.
I am delighted to have it so unexpectedly restored to
me. It has been a great inconvenience being without
it all these years.

Jack.

(*In a pathetic voice.*) Miss Prism, more is restored
to you than this hand-bag. I was the baby you placed
in it.

Miss Prism.

(*Amazed.*) You?

Jack.

(*Embracing her.*) Yes ... mother!

Miss Prism.

(*Recoiling in indignant astonishment.*) Mr. Worthing.
I am unmarried!

Jack.

Unmarried! I do not deny that is a serious blow. But
after all, who has the right to cast a stone against
one who has suffered? Cannot repentance wipe out
an act of folly? Why should there be one law for
men, and another for women? Mother, I forgive you.
(*Tries to embrace her again.*)

Miss Prism.

(*Still more indignant.*) Mr Worthing, there is some
error. (*Pointing to* LADY BRACKNELL.) There is
the lady who can tell you who you really are.

Jack.

(*After a pause.*) Lady Bracknell, I hate to seem in-
quisitive, but would you kindly inform me who I
am?

Lady Bracknell.

I am afraid that the news I have to give you will
not altogether please you. You are the son of my
poor sister, Mrs Moncrieff, and consequently Algernon's elder brother.

Jack.

Algy's elder brother! Then I have a brother after all.
I knew I had a brother! I always said I had a
brother! Cecily—how could you have ever doubted
that I had a brother? (*Seizes hold of* ALGERNON.)

Dr Chasuble, my unfortunate brother. Miss Prism, my unfortunate brother. Gwendolen, my unfortunate brother. Algy, you young scoundrel, you will have to treat me with more respect in the future. You have never behaved to me like a brother in all your life.

Algernon.
Well, not till to-day, old boy, I admit. I did my best, however, though I was out of practice.

(Shakes hands.)

Gwendolen.
(*To* JACK.) My own! But what own are you? What is your Christian name, now that you have become some one else?

Jack.
Good heavens! ... I had quite forgotten that point. Your decision on the subject of my name is irrevocable, I suppose?

Gwendolen.
I never change, except in my affections.

Cecily.
What a noble nature you have, Gwendolen!

Jack.
Then the question had better be cleared up at once. Aunt Augusta, a moment. At the time when Miss Prism left me in the hand-bag, had I been christened already?

Lady Bracknell.
Every luxury that money could buy, including christening, had been lavished on you by your fond and doting parents.

Jack.
Then I was christened! That is settled. Now, what name was I given? Let me know the worst.

Lady Bracknell.
Being the eldest son you were naturally christened after your father.

Jack.
(*Irritably.*) Yes, but what was my father's Christian name?

Lady Bracknell.
(*Meditatively.*) I cannot at the present moment recall

what the General's Christian name was. But I have
no doubt he had one. He was eccentric, I admit. But
only in later years. And that was the result of the
Indian climate, and marriage, and indigestion, and
other things of that kind.

Jack.

Algy! Can't you recollect what our father's Christian
name was?

Algernon.

My dear boy, we were never even on speaking
terms. He died before I was a year old.

Jack.

His name would appear in the Army Lists of the
period, I suppose, Aunt Augusta?

Lady Bracknell.

The General was essentially a man of peace, except
in his domestic life. But I have no doubt his name
would appear in any military directory.

Jack.

The Army Lists of the last forty years are here. These
delightful records should have been my constant
study. (*Rushes to bookcase and tears the books out.*)
M. Generals . . . Mallam, Maxbohm, Magley—what
ghastly names they have—Markby, Migsby, Mobbs,
Moncrieff! Lieutenant 1840, Captain, Lieutenant-
Colonel, Colonel, General 1869, Christian names,
Ernest John. (*Puts book very quietly down and speaks
quite calmly.*) I always told you, Gwendolen, my
name was Ernest, didn't I? Well, it is Ernest after all.
I mean it naturally is Ernest.

Lady Bracknell.

Yes, I remember now that the General was called
Ernest. I knew I had some particular reason for dis-
liking the name.

Gwendolen.

Ernest! My own Ernest! I felt from the first that
you could have no other name!

Jack.

Gwendolen, it is a terrible thing for a man to find
out suddenly that all his life he has been speaking
nothing but the truth. Can you forgive me?

Gwendolen.
I can. For I feel that you are sure to change.

Jack.
My own one!

Chasuble.
(*To* MISS PRISM.) Laetitia! (*Embraces her.*)

Miss Prism.
(*Enthusiastically.*) Frederick! At last!

Algernon.
Cecily! (*Embraces her.*) At last!

Jack.
Gwendolen! (*Embraces her.*) At last!

Lady Bracknell.
My nephew, you seem to be displaying signs of triviality.

Jack.
On the contrary, Aunt Augusta, I've now realized for the first time in my life the vital Importance of Being Earnest.

TABLEAU

CURTAIN

From Wilde's Letters

To George Alexander

[? July 1894]

The real charm of the play, if it is to have a charm, must be in the dialogue. The plot is slight, but, I think, adequate.... Well, I think an amusing thing with lots of fun and wit might be made. If you think so too, and care to have the refusal of it, do let me know, and send me £150. If when the play is finished, you think it too slight—not serious enough—of course you can have the £150 back. I want to go away and write it, and it could be ready in October, as I have nothing else to do.... In the meanwhile, my dear Aleck, I am so pressed for money that I don't know what to do. Of course I am extravagant. You have always been a good wise friend to me, so think what you can do.

To Lord Alfred Douglas

[? August 1894]   *5 Esplanade, Worthing*

I have been doing nothing here but bathing and playwriting. My play is really very funny: I am quite delighted with it. But it is not shaped yet. It lies in Sibylline leaves about the room, and Arthur has twice made a chaos of it by "tidying up." The result, however, was rather dramatic. I am inclined to think that Chaos is a stronger evidence for an Intelligent Creator than Kosmos is: the view might be expanded.

To Charles Spurrier Mason

[*August 1894*]   *5 Esplanade, Worthing*
My dear Charlie, Thanks for your letter. I am in a very much worse state for money than I told you. But am just finishing a new play which, as it is quite nonsensical and has no serious interest, will I hope bring me in a lot of red gold.

To Grace Hawthorne

[*Postmark 4 October 1894*]   *5 Esplanade, Worthing*
Dear Miss Hawthorne, My plays are difficult plays to produce well: they require artistic setting on the stage, a good company that knows something of the style essential to high comedy, beautiful dresses, a sense of the luxury of modern life, and unless you are going out with a management that is able to pay well for things that are worth paying for, and to spend money in suitable presentation, it would be much better for you not to think of producing my plays. The very nominal sum I said I would accept in advance of fees I would not, I need hardly say, have accepted from anyone else: but as you said you were in some difficulty I was ready to take a nominal sum in advance. A management that could not pay that could not, I fear, give anything better than a travesty of my work. Some day you must find a brilliant manager who can

produce things well for you. I will be charmed then
to have a talk with you over some play of mine.

To George Alexander

[*Circa 25 October 1894*]   *16 Tite Street*
My dear Aleck, I have been ill in bed for a long time,
with a sort of malarial fever, and have not been able
to answer your kind letter of invitation. I am quite well
now, and, as you wished to see my somewhat farcical
comedy, I send you the first copy of it. It is called
Lady Lancing on the cover: but the real title is *The
Importance of Being Earnest.* When you read the play,
you will see the punning title's meaning. Of course,
the play is not suitable to you at all: you are a romantic actor: the people it wants are actors like Wyndham
and Hawtrey. Also, I would be sorry if you altered
the definite artistic line of progress you have always followed at the St James's. But, of course, read it, and
let me know what you think about it. I have very good
offers from America for it.

To Arthur L. Humphreys

[*Circa 12 February 1895*]   *Hotel Avondale, Piccadilly*
My dear Humphreys, I enclose you a stall for Thursday—the last to be got! I hope you will enjoy my
"trivial" play. It is written by a butterfly for butterflies.

FOUR-ACT VERSION

New York Public Library Text

From ACT ONE

Algernon.
... My experience of life is that whenever one tells a lie one is corroborated on every side. When one tells the truth one is left in a very lonely and painful position, and no one believes a word one says. ...

* * *

Lady Brancaster.
... But I don't think, Algernon, I could possibly leave Gwendolen and Mr. Worthing alone. ... You see, like most people whom one meets everywhere, one doesn't know anything about him. And he seems to be paying considerable attentions to Gwendolen, who I regret to say does not treat him with the marked coldness that—

Algernon.
Oh! that is all right, Aunt Augusta. He is not at all in love with her. He was just telling me so when you came in. The fact simply is that they are both very much interested in questions like the "Better housing of the upper classes," [and] "The bringing of Culture within the easy reach of the rich."

Lady Brancaster.
Ah! those are subjects that I do not consider at all dangerous. ... They are not in any way practical.

Gwendolen, I am going with Algernon into the music-room for a moment to expurgate the programme for Saturday night. I should like your father to be able to be present.... I will see you again, no doubt, Mr. Worthing.

(JACK *bows. Exit* LADY BRANCASTER *with* ALGERNON.)

Jack.
I would like, Miss Fairfax, to take advantage of Lady Brancaster's temporary absence.
Gwendolen.
Yes, Mr. Worthing, I would certainly advise you to do so.
Jack.
(*A little taken aback.*) Ahem! ... I hope that what I am going to say to you will not be in any way a shock to you.
Gwendolen.
Oh! I am sure it won't. I have never been shocked in my life. I think to be shocked by anything shows a very low ethical standard. Nobody is ever shocked now-a-days except the clergy and the middle classes. It is the profession of the one and the punishment of the other.

* * *

Lady Brancaster.
Surname, Worthing?
Jack.
Yes.
Lady Brancaster.
I think that Worthing-Worthing with a hyphen would be better. I have known a hyphen produce a wonderful social effect, when judiciously used. However, that point can stand over for the present....

* * *

Lady Brancaster.
Indeed, I do not think that under any circumstances

the "Morning Post" could possibly notice you, although that paper has become sadly democratic lately; which is strange, as it is only a few years since it lowered its price in order to suit the diminished incomes of the aristocracy.

Jack.
My dear Lady Brancaster, to speak to you candidly, I don't care twopence whether the "Morning Post" notices me or not. Who on earth would care?

Lady Brancaster.
The price of the paper is, I am glad to say, merely one penny. And, if you will allow me to say so, I am sorry, for your own sake, to hear you speak in slighting terms of that admirable journal. It is the only document of our time from which the history of the English people in the XIXth century could be written with any regard to decorum or even decency. (*Rises to go.*)

* * *

Algernon.
Oh, no good chap makes a good husband. If a chap makes a good husband there must have been something rather peculiar about him when he was a bachelor. To be a good husband requires considerable practice.

* * *

Algernon.
And what did Aunt Augusta say?

Jack.
Oh, she was positively violent. I never heard such language in the whole course of my life from anyone. She might just as well have been in a pulpit. I shouldn't be at all surprised if she took to philanthropy or something of the sort and abused her fellow creatures for the rest of her life.

* * *

Jack.

. . . And after all what does it matter whether a man has ever had a father and mother or not? Mothers, of course, are all right. They pay a chap's bills and don't bother him. But father's bother a chap and never pay his bills. I don't know a single chap at the club who speaks to his father.

From ACT TWO

Chasuble.

Reading Political Economy, Cecily? It is wonderful how girls are educated now-a-days. I suppose you know all about the relations between Capital and Labour. I wish I did. I am compelled, like most of my brother clergy, to treat scientific subjects from the point of view of sentiment. But that is more impressive I think. Accurate knowledge is out of place in a pulpit. It is secular.

* * *

Cecily.

. . . Miss Prism and I lunch at 2 off some roast mutton.

Algernon.

I fear that would be too rich for me.

Cecily.

Uncle Jack, whose health has been sadly undermined by the late hours you keep in town, has been ordered by his London doctor to have *pâté-de-foie-gras* sandwiches and 1874 champagne at 12. I don't know if such invalid's fare would suit you.

Algernon.

You are sure the champagne is '74?

Cecily.

Poor Uncle Jack has not been allowed to drink anything else for the last two years. Even the cheaper clarets are, he tells me, strictly forbidden to him.

Merriman.
(*To* ERNEST.) I beg your pardon, sir, there is an elderly gentleman wishes to see you. He has just come in a cab from the station. (*Hands card on salver.*)

Algernon.
To see me?

Merriman.
Yes, sir.

Algernon.
(*Reads card.*) "Parker and Gribsby, Solicitors." I don't know anything about them. Who are they?

Jack.
(*Takes card.*) Parker and Gribsby. I wonder who they can be. I expect, Ernest, they have come about some business for your friend Bunbury. Perhaps Bunbury wants to make his will, and wishes you to be executor. (*To* MERRIMAN.) Show Messrs. Parker and Gribsby in at once.

Merriman.
There is only one gentleman in the hall, sir.

Jack.
Show either Mr. Parker or Mr. Gribsby in.

Merriman.
Yes, sir. (*Exit.*)

Jack.
I hope, Ernest, that I may rely on the statement you made to me last week when I finally settled all your bills for you. I hope you have no outstanding accounts of any kind.

Algernon.
I haven't any debts at all, dear Jack. Thanks to your generosity I don't owe a penny, except for a few neckties I believe.

Jack.
I am sincerely glad to hear it.

Merriman.
Mr. Gribsby. (*Enter* GRIBSBY.)

Gribsby.
(*To* CANON CHASUBLE.) Mr. Ernest Worthing?

Miss Prism.
This is Mr. Ernest Worthing.

Gribsby.
Mr. Ernest Worthing?

Algernon.
Yes.

Gribsby.
Of B.4, the Albany—?

Algernon.
Yes, that is my address.

Gribsby.
I am very sorry, Mr. Worthing, but we have a writ of attachment for 20 days against you at the suit of the Savoy Hotel Co. Limited for £762.14.2.

Algernon.
What perfect nonsense! I never dine at the Savoy at my own expense. I always dine at Willis's. It is far more expensive. I don't owe a penny to the Savoy.

Gribsby.
The writ is marked as having been on you personally at the Albany on May the 27th. Judgment was given in default against you on the fifth of June. Since then we have written to you no less than thirteen times, without receiving any reply. In the interest of our clients we had no option but to obtain an order for committal of your person. But, no doubt, Mr. Worthing, you will be able to settle the account without any further unpleasantness. Seven and six should be added to the bill of costs for expense of the cab which was hired for your convenience in case of any necessity of removal, but that, I am sure, is a contingency that is not likely to occur.

Algernon.
Removal! What on earth do you mean by removal? I haven't the smallest intention of going away. I am staying here for a week. I am staying with my brother. (*Points to* JACK.)

Gribsby.
(*To* JACK.) Pleased to meet you, sir.

Algernon.
(*To* GRIBSBY.) If you imagine I am going up to town the moment I arrive you are extremely mistaken.

Gribsby.
I am merely a solicitor myself. I do not employ personal violence of any kind. The officer of the court

whose function it is to seize the person of the debtor is waiting in the fly outside. He has considerable experience in these matters. In the point of fact he has arrested in the course of his duties nearly all the younger sons of the aristocracy, as well as several eldest sons, besides of course a good many members of the House of Lords. His style and manner are considered extremely good. Indeed, he looks more like a betting man than a court-official. That is why we always employ him. But no doubt you will prefer to pay the bill.

Algernon.
Pay it? How on earth am I going to do that? You don't suppose I have got any money? How perfectly silly you are. No gentleman ever has any money.

Gribsby.
My experience is that it is usually relatives who pay.

Jack.
Kindly allow me to see this bill, Mr. Gribsby ... (*Turns over immense folio.*) ... £762.14.2 since last October. ... I am bound to say I never saw such reckless extravagance in all my life. (*Hands it to DR. CHASUBLE.*)

Miss Prism.
762 pounds for eating! How grossly materialistic! There can be little good in any young man who eats so much, and so often.

Chasuble.
It certainly is a painful proof of the disgraceful luxury of the age. We are far away from Wordsworth's plain living and high thinking.

Jack.
Now, Dr. Chasuble, do you consider that I am in any way called upon to pay this monstrous account for my brother?

Chasuble.
I am bound to say that I do not think so. It would be encouraging his profligacy.

Miss Prism.
As a man sows, so let him reap. This proposed incarceration might be most salutary. It is to be regretted that [it] is only for 20 days.

Jack.

I am quite of your opinion.

Algernon.

My dear fellow, how ridiculous you are! You know perfectly well that the bill is really yours.

Jack.

Mine?

Algernon.

Yes, you know it is.

Chasuble.

Mr. Worthing, if this is a jest, it is out of place.

Miss Prism.

It is gross effrontery. Just what I expected from him.

Cecily.

It is ingratitude. I didn't expect that.

Jack.

Never mind what he says. This is the way he always goes on. You mean now to say that you are not Ernest Worthing, residing at B.4, The Albany? I wonder, as you are at it, that you don't deny being my brother at all. Why don't you?

Algernon.

Oh! I am not going to do that, my dear fellow; it would be absurd. Of course, I'm your brother. And that is why you should pay this bill for me. What is the use of having a brother, if he doesn't pay one's bills for one?

Jack.

Personally, if you ask me, I don't see any use in having a brother. As for paying your bill, I have not the smallest intention of doing anything of the kind. Dr. Chasuble, the worthy Rector of this parish, and Miss Prism, in whose admirable and sound judgment I place great reliance, are both of opinion that incarceration would do you a great deal of good. And I think so, too.

Gribsby.

(*Pulls out watch.*) I am sorry to disturb this pleasant family meeting, but time presses. We have to be at Holloway not later than four o'clock; otherwise it is difficult to obtain admission. The rules are very strict.

Algernon.

Holloway!

Gribsby.
It is at Holloway that detentions of this character take
place always.

Algernon.
Well, I really am not going to be imprisoned in the
suburbs for having dined in the West End. It is perfectly ridiculous.

Gribsby.
The bill is for suppers, not for dinners.

Algernon.
I really don't care. All I say is that I am not going
to be imprisoned in the suburbs.

Gribsby.
The surroundings, I admit, are middle class; but the
gaol itself is fashionable and well-aired, and there are
ample opportunities of taking exercise at certain
stated hours of the day. In the case of a medical certi-
ficate, which is always easy to obtain, the hours can
be extended.

Algernon.
Exercise! Good God! No gentleman ever takes exercise. You don't seem to understand what a gentleman
is.

Gribsby.
I have met so many of them, sir, that I am afraid
I don't. There are the most curious varieties of them.
The result of cultivation, no doubt. Will you kindly
come now, sir, if it will not be inconvenient to you.

Algernon.
(*Appealingly.*) Jack!

Miss Prism.
Pray be firm, Mr. Worthing.

Chasuble.
This is an occasion on which any weakness would
be out of place. It would be a form of self-deception.

Jack.
I am quite firm; and I don't know what weakness
or deception of any kind is.

Cecily.
Uncle Jack! I think you have a little money of mine,
haven't you? Let me pay this bill. I wouldn't like
your own brother to be in prison.

Jack.

Oh, you can't pay it, Cecily, that is nonsense.

Cecily.

Then you will, won't you? I think you would be sorry if you thought your own brother was shut up. Of course, I am quite disappointed with him.

Jack.

You won't speak to him again, Cecily, will you?

Cecily.

Certainly not, unless, of course, he speaks to me first; it would be very rude not to answer him.

Jack.

Well, I'll take care he doesn't speak to you. I'll take care he doesn't speak to anybody in this house. The man should be cut, Mr. Gribsby——

Gribsby.

Yes, sir.

Jack.

I'll pay this bill for my brother. It is the last bill I shall ever pay for him, too. How much is it?

Gribsby.

£762.14.2. May I ask your full name, sir?

Jack.

Mr. John Worthing J.P., The Manor House, Woolton. Does that satisfy you?

Gribsby.

Oh, certainly, sir, certainly! It was a mere formality. (*To* MISS PRISM.) Handsome place. Ah! the cab will be 5/9 extra—hired for the convenience of the client.

Jack.

All right.

Miss Prism.

I must say that I think such generosity quite foolish. Especially paying the cab.

Chasuble.

(*With a wave of the hand.*) The heart has its wisdom as well as the head, Miss Prism.

Jack.

Payable to Gribsby and Parker, I suppose.

Gribsby.

Yes, sir. Kindly don't cross the cheque. Thank you.

Jack.

You are Gribsby, aren't you? What is Parker like?

Gribsby.
I am both, sir. Gribsby when I am on unpleasant business, Parker on occasions of a less serious kind.

Jack.
The next time I see you I hope you will be Parker.

Gribsby.
I hope so, sir. (*To* DR. CHASUBLE.) Good day. (DR. CHASUBLE *bows coldly.*) Good day. (MISS PRISM *bows coldly.*) Hope I shall have the pleasure of meeting you again. (*To* ALGERNON.)

Algernon.
I sincerely hope not. What ideas you have of the sort of society a gentleman wants to mix in. No gentleman ever wants to know a solicitor who wants to imprison one in the suburbs.

Gribsby.
Quite so, quite so.

Algernon.
By the way, Gribsby. Gribsby, you are not to go back to the station in that cab. That is my cab. It was taken for my convenience. You and the gentleman who looks like the betting-man have got to walk to the station. And a very good thing, too. Solicitors don't walk nearly enough. They bolt. But they don't walk. I don't know any solicitor who takes sufficient exercise. As a rule they sit in stuffy offices all day long neglecting their business.

Jack.
You can take the cab, Mr. Gribsby.

Gribsby.
Thank you, sir. (*Exit.*)

Algernon.
Well, I must say that I think you might have let me play my joke on Gribsby. It was rather a good joke in its way. And of course I wasn't serious about it.

From ACT THREE

Jack.
. . . I am sorry you have forced me to speak the thing right out. I would have wished personally,

Gwendolen, for your sake as well as for my own, to have broken the thing gently to you. It had always been my intention to do so.

Gwendolen.
Broken it gently to me! As if John was a name that could be broken gently to anyone. I had no idea you were so cynical.

Algernon.
I would like to say, Miss Cardew, that I regret you insisted on a frank answer to your question. I had hoped to have found an opportunity of gradually leading up to the name of Algernon.

Cecily.
As if one could gradually lead up to Algernon. I am afraid, Mr. Montford, you are little more than a mere sentimentalist. A type I have but little respect for, common though it is at the end of this, as of every century.

From ACT FOUR

Merriman.
Ahem! Ahem! Lady Brancaster!

Jack.
Good heavens! The Gorgon!

Gwendolen.
My mother!

Algernon.
My aunt!

(GWENDOLEN *clings to* JACK. ALGERNON *disappears with* CECILY *behind a screen l.c. and remains in full sight of the audience.* ALGERNON *makes signs to* CECILY *to keep quite still, and from time to time says "Hush!"*)

* * *

Algernon.
(*To* CECILY *behind screen.*) Hush!

Lady Brancaster.
(*Looks round again at* GWENDOLEN *and* JACK

with troubled expression, then proceeds.) The painful circumstances of your origin, Mr. Worthing, make you, as I am sure you will frankly admit yourself, quite impossible as a suitor for the hand of Lord Brancaster's only child, and mine.

Jack.

I am engaged to be married to Gwendolen, Lady Brancaster!

Lady Brancaster.

You are nothing of the kind, sir. Nor have you any right to make such a statement in the presence of her mother, whose decision in this matter, as in all matters indeed, is final. Gwendolen, we will return to town at once. Tomorrow I will make arrangements for taking you abroad. I am going to order your father to Carlsbad; and a course of those saline waters would I think have a chastening effect on your foolish attempts at independence. In your father's case, at any rate, I have never found them fail. And your conduct to-day reminds me somewhat of his own behaviour in the early days of our happy married life.

Algernon.

(*Behind screen to* CECILY *who is whispering and laughing.*) Hush!

Lady Brancaster.

Mr. Worthing, is it you who keeps on saying "Hush" whenever I am talking?

Jack.

No, Lady Brancaster. I have been listening with the deepest interest to everything you say.

Lady Brancaster.

It is clear then that there is someone who says "Hush" concealed in this apartment. The ejaculation has reached my ears more than once. It is not at any time a very refined expression, and its use, when I am talking, is extremely vulgar, and indeed insolent. I suspect it to have proceeded from the lips of someone who is of more than usually low origin.

Jack.

I really think you must be mistaken about it, Lady Brancaster. There is a sort of echo I believe in this room. I have no doubt it is that.

Lady Brancaster.
(*With a bitter smile.*) In the course of my travels I have visited many of the localities most remarkable for their echoes, both at home and abroad. I am ready to admit that the accuracy of their powers of repetition has been grossly overestimated, no doubt for the sake of gain, but in no instance have I ever found an echo to say "Hush" in answer to an observation. Such an occurrence would be most improper. It would be a kind of miracle. It would tend to superstition. My hearing, I may mention, is unusually acute, as indeed are all my senses: my sight, my touch, my capacity for discerning odours. (*Looks about room carefully with her lorgnette. Finally, catching sight of a glance between* JACK *and* GWENDOLEN, *she turns her attention to the screen. She glares at it for a short time.*) Mr. Worthing, might I ask you to be kind enough to move aside that screen?

Jack.
(*Cheerily.*) What screen, Lady Brancaster?

Lady Brancaster.
(*Stonily.*) That screen, if you please. I see no other in the room. (JACK *is obliged to move back the screen.* ALGERNON *and* CECILY *are discovered; they are holding each other's hands.*)

* * *

Jack.
It pains me very much to have to speak frankly to you, Lady Brancaster, about your nephew, but the fact is that I do not approve at all of his moral character. In fact, I suspect him of being untruthful.

(ALGERNON *and* CECILY *look at him in amazement.*)

Lady Brancaster.
Untruthful! My nephew Algernon? Impossible!

Jack.
He obtained admission into my house, into my home-circle indeed, under the false pretence of being my brother. Under an assumed name he drank an entire

bottle of my '74 champagne, a wine I was specially reserving for myself. Continuing his disgraceful deception, he succeeded in the course of the afternoon in alienating the affections of my only ward. He subsequently stayed to tea. And what makes his conduct all the more heartless is, that he was perfectly well aware from the first that I have no brother, and that I never had a brother, not even of any kind. I distinctly told him so myself in Half Moon Street, yesterday.

Cecily.
But, dear Uncle Jack, you informed us all that you had a brother. You dwelt continually on the subject. Algy merely corroborated your statement. It was noble of him.

Jack.
Pardon me, Cecily, you are a little too young to understand these matters. To invent anything at all is an act of sheer genius, and, in a commercial age like ours, shows considerable physical courage——Few of our modern novelists ever dare to invent a single thing. It is an open secret that they don't know how to do it. Upon the other hand, to corroborate a lie is a distinctly cowardly action. I know it is a thing that the newspapers do one for the other, every day. But it is not the act of a gentleman. No gentleman ever corroborates a thing that he knows to be untrue.

Algernon.
(*Furiously.*) Jack! I never heard such a thing in my life. I really won't stand it.

Jack.
(*With a pained look.*) A moment, Algernon. Nor is this all, Lady Brancaster, worse remains behind.

Lady Brancaster.
My experience of life is that it usually does. . . . But proceed, Mr. Worthing, in your story. I need not tell you how much it distresses me. I shall certainly consider it my painful duty to conceal all the facts from Lord Brancaster. Fortunately, it has been my habit to do that for years. Indeed I may say that he never knows about anything that occurs to any single mem-

ber of his family. Proceed, Mr. Worthing. I am listening with all an aunt's natural anxiety.

Jack.
At two o'clock this afternoon, Lady Brancaster, in order to save your nephew from immediate imprisonment, I paid for him out of my own pocket bills amounting to £376.14.2. I think it right to add that these bills showed on the surface that they were contracted by one whose life was more than usually reckless and extravagant. The two chief creditors were the Willis Restaurant, and Mr. Arundel, the jeweller of Bond Street. We all know what that ends in. . . . I think, Lady Brancaster, that now that you see that but for my intervention your nephew would at this moment be leading the luxurious and indolent existence of a first-class misdemeanant, you will realize how impossible I find it to entrust to so weak and foolish a character the care of the future happiness of my dear ward. (*Rings bell. Enter* MERRIMAN.) Some sherry, please.

Merriman.
Yes, sir. (*Exit.*)

Lady Brancaster.
I can only promise you, Mr. Worthing, that these unfortunate incidents will be carefully kept from Lord Brancaster.

Algernon.
(*After a whisper with* CECILY.) My dear fellow, you are playing it a little too high, aren't you? I don't think I can quite pass that. Aunt Augusta, it is only fair to myself to tell you that the bills weren't mine at all, they were his. I had nothing whatsoever to do with them.

(*Enter* MERRIMAN *with sherry.* JACK *takes a glass.*)

Jack.
I had hoped, Algernon, to have spared you the necessity of making that painful confession. In the eyes of any sensible person, it puts your conduct in a light that is, if possible, still more disgraceful. As, however,

you have chosen yourself to make the matter public, you must bear the necessary consequences. (ALGERNON *approaches table where the sherry is.* JACK *removes the decanter to a table behind him. r.f.*) Your nephew, Lady Brancaster, as he has just admitted himself, compelled me at 2 o'clock this afternoon to pay my own bills, a thing I have not done for years, a thing that is strictly against my principles, a thing that I in every way disapprove of. In taking that attitude, I am not merely speaking for myself, but for others. More young men are ruined now-a-days by paying their bills than by anything else. I know many fashionable young men in London, young men of rank and position, whose rooms are absolutely littered with receipts, and who, with a callousness that seems to me absolutely cynical, have no hesitation in paying ready money for the mere luxuries of life. Such conduct seems to me to strike at the very foundation of things. The only basis for good Society is unlimited credit. Without that, Society, as we know it, crumbles. Why is it that we all despise the middle classes? Simply because they invariably pay what they owe. . . . You are now in full possession of the sad details about your nephew's conduct, Lady Brancaster. I hope you will lay them before Lord Brancaster on your return to town, and ask his opinion about them. (*Drinks sherry.*)

Lady Brancaster.
I think I shall. It might be too great a shock to Lord Brancaster to be asked his opinion about anything. . . . Ahem! Ahem. . . . Algernon, pray be more reposeful. (*To* ALGERNON *who is consoling* CECILY.) You are much too demonstrative, and demonstrations of any kind are extremely vulgar and democratic. We have far too many of them, now-a-days, as it is. I am told that Hyde Park, on the one day of the week on which one doesn't want to use it, is quite unbearable. . . . Ahem! Mr. Worthing, after careful consideration I have decided to overlook my nephew's conduct— painful to you though it undoubtedly has been. Cec-

ily, I still consent to your engagement with Algernon. Indeed, I may say that I insist upon it. When my heart is touched, I become like granite. Nothing can move me.

Cecily.
Thank you, Aunt Augusta.

Jack.
Cecily, your addressing Lady Brancaster as your Aunt Augusta is not merely historically inaccurate, but expresses a disregard of your kind guardian's wise decision about your future life which both surprises and wounds me.

Cecily.
Uncle Jack! An expression that I may mention is historically inaccurate. I think you are perfectly horrid! I can't understand you.

Jack.
Young girls are not expected to understand very abstruse problems.

Cecily.
I don't think you are an abstruse problem at all. I simply think you are very cruel, and so unreasonable that I suspect you of being a fallacy of some kind.

Jack.
Believe me, dear Cecily, I am acting for the best.

Cecily
People always say that when they do their worst.

Jack.
Child! Who taught you such a pessimistic idea?

Cecily
No one; if I had been taught it, I wouldn't believe it.

* * *

Jack.
. . . What is a selfish person? A selfish person is surely one who seeks to keep his joys and sorrows to himself. I am not like that. When I am unhappy, as I am now, I desire everyone to share in my unhappiness. I give freely of my misfortunes. I do not treat my misery as a miser treats his gold. On the contrary, I scatter it abroad with a lavish hand. If I am blighted

there is a general blight, and no one can complain
that they are left out or overlooked.

Cecily.

Gwendolen, will you appeal to him.

Gwendolen.

I will be very glad indeed to tell him what I think
of his conduct. (*Goes over to* JACK.) . . . Up to the
present moment I will frankly admit that I have
always admired you. Now I simply adore you. It requires merely physical courage to sacrifice oneself.
To sacrifice others moral courage is necessary.

AN OLD NEW PLAY

George Bernard Shaw

The Importance of Being Earnest. A trivial comedy for serious people. By Oscar Wilde. St James's Theatre, 14 February 1895.

[*23 February 1895*]

It is somewhat surprising to find Mr Oscar Wilde, who does not usually model himself on Mr Henry Arthur Jones, giving his latest play a five-chambered title like The Case of Rebellious Susan. So I suggest with some confidence that The Importance of Being Earnest dates from a period long anterior to Susan. However it may have been retouched immediately before its production, it must certainly have been written before Lady Windermere's Fan. I do not suppose it to be Mr Wilde's first play: he is too susceptible to fine art to have begun otherwise than with a strenuous imitation of a great dramatic poem, Greek or Shakespearean; but it was perhaps the first which he designed for practical commercial use at the West End theatres. The evidence of this is abundant. The play has a plot —a gross anachronism; there is a scene between the two girls in the second act quite in the literary style of Mr Gilbert, and almost inhuman enough to have been conceived by him; the humor is adulterated by stock mechanical fun to an extent that absolutely scandalizes one in a play with such an author's name to it; and the punning title and several of the more farcical passages recall the epoch of the late H. J. Byron.

The whole has been varnished, and here and there veneered, by the author of A Woman of No Importance; but the general effect is that of a farcical comedy dating from the seventies, unplayed during that period because it was too clever and too decent, and brought up to date as far as possible by Mr Wilde in his now completely formed style. Such is the impression left by the play on me. But I find other critics, equally entitled to respect, declaring that The Importance of Being Earnest is a strained effort of Mr Wilde's at ultramodernity, and that it could never have been written but for the opening up of entirely new paths in drama last year by Arms and the Man. At which I confess to a chuckle.

I cannot say that I greatly cared for The Importance of Being Earnest. It amused me, of course; but unless comedy touches me as well as amuses me, it leaves me with a sense of having wasted my evening. I go to the theatre to be moved to laughter, not to be tickled or bustled into it; and that is why, though I laugh as much as anybody at a farcical comedy, I am out of spirits before the end of the second act, and out of temper before the end of the third, my miserable mechanical laughter intensifying these symptoms at every outburst. If the public ever becomes intelligent enough to know when it is really enjoying itself and when it is not, there will be an end of farcical comedy. Now in The Importance of Being Earnest there is plenty of this rib-tickling: for instance, the lies, the deceptions, the cross purposes, the sham mourning, the christening of the two grown-up men, the muffin eating, and so forth. These could only have been raised from the farcical plane by making them occur to characters who had, like Don Quixote, convinced us of their reality and obtained some hold on our sympathy. But that unfortunate moment of Gilbertism breaks our belief in the humanity of the play. Thus we are thrown back on the force and daintiness of its wit, brought home by an exquisitely grave, natural, and unconscious execution on the part of the actors. Alas! the latter is not forthcoming. Mr Kinsey Peile as a man-servant, and Miss Irene Vanbrugh as Gwendolen Fairfax, alone escaped from a devastating consciousness of Mr Wilde's reputation, which more or less preoccupied all the rest, except perhaps Miss Millard, with whom all comedy is a preoccupation, since she is essentially a sentimental actress. In such passages as the Gilbertian quarrel with Gwendolen, her charm rebuked the scene instead of enhancing it. The older ladies were, if they will excuse my saying so, quite maddening. The violence of their affectation, the insufferable low comedy soars and swoops of the voice, the rigid shivers of elbow, shoulder, and neck, which are supposed on the stage to characterize the behavior of ladies after the age of forty, played havoc with the piece. In Miss Rose Leclerq a good deal of this sort of thing is only the mannerism of a genuine if somewhat impossible style; but Miss Leclerq was absent through indisposition on the night of my visit; so that I had not her style to console me. Mr Aynesworth's easy-going Our Boys style of play suited his part rather happily; and Mr Alexander's graver and more refined manner made the right contrast with it. But Mr Alexander, after playing with very nearly if not quite perfect conviction in the first two acts, suddenly lost confidence in the third, and began to spur up for a rattling finish. From the moment that began, the play was done with. The speech in which Worthing forgives his supposed mother, and the business of searching the army lists, which should have been conducted with subdued earnestness, was bustled through to the destruction of all verisimilitude and consequently all interest. That is the worst of having anyone who is not an inveterate and hardened comedian in a leading comedy part. His faith, patience, and relish begin to give out after a time; and he finally commits the unpardonable sin against the author of giving the signal that the play is over ten minutes before the fall of the curtain, instead of speaking the last line as if the whole evening were still before the audience. Mr Alexander does not throw himself genuinely into comedy: he condescends to amuse himself with it; and in the end he finds that he cannot condescend enough. On the whole I must decline to accept The Importance of Being Earnest as a day less than ten years old; and I am altogether unable to perceive any uncommon excellence in its presentation.

"THE IMPORTANCE OF BEING EARNEST"

Max Beerbohm

[*January 18, 1902*]

Of a play representing actual life there can be, I think, no test more severe than its revival after seven or eight years of abeyance. For that period is enough to make it untrue to the surface of the present, yet not enough to enable us to unswitch it from the present. How seldom is the test passed! There is a better chance, naturally, for plays that weave life into fantastic forms; but even for them not a very good chance; for the fashion in fantasy itself changes. Fashions form a cycle, and we, steadily moving in that cycle, are farther from whatever fashion we have just passed than from any other. The things which once pleased our grandfathers are tolerable in comparison with the things which once pleased us. If in the lumber of the latter we find something that still pleases us, pleases us as much as ever it did, then, surely, we may preen ourselves on the possession of a classic, and congratulate posterity. Last week, at the St. James', was revived "The Importance of Being Earnest," after an abeyance of exactly seven years—those seven years which, according to scientists, change every molecule in the human body, leaving nothing of what was there before. And yet to me the play came out fresh and exquisite as ever, and over the whole house almost every line was sending ripples of laughter—cumulative ripples that became waves, and receded only for fear of drowning the next line. In kind the play always was unlike any other, and in its kind it still seems perfect. I do not wonder that now the critics boldly call it a classic, and predict immortality. And (timorous though I am apt to be in prophecy) I join gladly in their chorus.

A classic must be guarded jealously. Nothing should be added to, or detracted from, a classic. In the revival at the St. James', I noted several faults of textual omission. When Lady Bracknell is told by Mr. Worthing that he was originally found in a hand-bag in the cloakroom of Victoria Station, she echoes "The cloak-room at Victoria Station?" "Yes," he replies; "the Brighton Line." "The line is immaterial," she rejoins; "Mr. Worthing, I confess I am somewhat bewildered," &c., &c. Now, in the present revival "the line is immaterial" is omitted. Perhaps Mr. Alexander regarded it as an immaterial line. So it is, as far as the plot is concerned. But is not the less deliciously funny. To skip it is inexcusable. Again, Mr. Wilde was a master in selection of words, and his words must not be amended. "Cecily," says Miss Prism, "you will read your Political Economy in my absence. The chapter on the Fall of the Rupee you may omit. It is somewhat too sensational." For "sensational" Miss Laverton substitutes "exciting"—a very poor substitute for that *mot juste*. Thus may the edge of magnificent absurdity be blunted. In the last act, again, Miss Laverton killed a vital point by inaccuracy. In the whole play there is no more delicious speech than Miss Prism's rhapsody over the restored hand-bag. This is a speech quintessential of the whole play's spirit. "It seems to be mine," says Miss Prism calmly. "Yes, here is the injury it received through the upsetting of a Gower Street omnibus in younger and happier days. There is the stain on the lining caused by the explosion of a temperance beverage—an incident that occurred at Leamington. And here, on the lock, are my initials. I had forgotten that in an extravagant moment I had had them placed there.

The bag is undoubtedly mine. I am delighted to have it so unexpectedly restored to me. It has been a great inconvenience being without it all these years." The overturning of a Gower Street omnibus in younger and happier days! Miss Laverton omitted "and happier." What a point to miss! Moreover, she gabbled the whole speech, paying no heed to those well-balanced cadences whose dignity contributes so much to the fun—without whose dignity, indeed, the fun evaporates. In such a play as this good acting is peculiarly important. It is, also, peculiarly difficult to obtain. The play is unique in kind, and thus most of the mimes, having trained themselves for ordinary purposes, are bewildered in approaching it.

Before we try to define how it should be acted, let us try to define its character. In scheme, of course, it is a hackneyed farce—the story of a young man coming up to London "on the spree," and of another young man going down conversely to the country, and of the complications that ensue. In treatment, also, it is farcical, in so far as some of the fun depends on absurd "situations," "stage-business," and so forth. Thus one might assume that the best way to act it would be to rattle through it. That were a gross error. For, despite the scheme of the play, the fun depends mainly on what the characters say, rather than on what they do. They speak a kind of beautiful nonsense—the language of high comedy, twisted into fantasy. Throughout the dialogue is the horse-play of a distinguished intellect and a distinguished imagination—a horse-play among words and ideas, conducted with poetic dignity. What differentiates this farce from any other, and makes it funnier than any other, is the humorous contrast between its style and matter. To preserve its style fully, the dialogue must be spoken with grave unction. The sound and the sense of the words must be taken seriously, treated beautifully. If mimes rattle through the play and anyhow, they manage to obscure much of its style, and much, therefore, of its fun. They lower it towards the plane of ordinary farce. This was what the mimes at the St. James' were doing on the first night. The play triumphed not by their help but in their despite. I must except Miss Lilian Braithwaite, who acted in precisely the right key of grace and dignity. She alone, in seeming to take her part quite seriously, showed that she had realised the full extent of its fun. Miss Margaret Halstan acted prettily, but in the direction of burlesque. By displaying a sense of humour she betrayed its limitations. Mr. Lyall Swete played the part of Doctor Chasuble as though it were a minutely realistic character study of a typical country clergyman. Instead of taking the part seriously for what it is, he tried to make it a serious part. He slurred over all the majestic utterances of the Canon, as though he feared that if he spoke them with proper unction he would be accused of forgetting that he was no longer in the Benson Company. I sighed for Mr. Henry Kemble, who "created" the part. I sighed, also, for the late Miss Rose Leclerq, who "created" the part of Lady Bracknell. Miss M. Talbot plays it in the conventional stage-dowager fashion. Miss Leclerq—but no! I will not sink without a struggle into that period when a man begins to bore young people by raving to them about the mimes whom they never saw. Both Mr. George Alexander and Mr. Graham Browne rattled through their parts. Even in the second act, when not only the situation, but also the necessity for letting the audience realise the situation, demands that John Worthing should make the slowest of entries, Mr. Alexander came bustling on at break-neck speed. I wish he would reconsider his theory of the play, call some rehearsals, and have his curtain rung up not at 8.45 but at 8.15. He may argue that this would not be worth his while, as *Paolo and Francesca* is to be produced so soon. I hope he is not going to have "Paolo and Francesca" rattled through. The effect on it would be quite as bad as on *The Importance of Being Earnest* —though not, I assure him, worse.

THE COLLECTED PLAYS
OF OSCAR WILDE

St. John Hankin

The complete edition of the works of Oscar Wilde, which Messrs. Methuen are now issuing under the editorship of Mr. Robert Ross, has a special interest for the student of the English drama of the latter part of the nineteenth century. For the first six volumes of it are devoted to the plays, and by their appearance one is now enabled for the first time to consider their author's dramatic work as a whole. Hitherto this has been impossible, since the early plays, *Vera, or the Nihilists* and *The Duchess of Padua,* and also the fragment of *A Florentine Tragedy*—which belongs in style to the early period though it was actually written comparatively late in his career—have never hitherto been either published or publicly performed in this country. *The Duchess of Padua* was originally produced in the United States, and has also been played, in a prose translation, in Germany, and both it and *Vera* have been printed in pirated editions in America and elsewhere. But seeing that the pirated edition of *Vera* was a careless and inaccurate reprint from a prompt copy, and that of *The Duchess of Padua* a prose translation of the German version—Wilde's play is in blank verse—it will be understood that not much help could be got from them by any one who desired to form a critical estimate of the plays, even if he were prepared to go to the trouble and expense of smuggling them.

This unsatisfactory state of things is now at an end. All the plays are now published in an authorised and unmutilated form, and though one cannot pretend that any of the three now printed for the first time are on a level with their author's best work, they have their importance for any one who wishes to understand Wilde as a dramatist and to estimate his powers and his limitations. On the whole, they certainly illustrate the limitations rather than the powers. Mr. Ross, in a characteristic dedicatory letter prefixed to *The Duchess of Padua,* acknowledges with engaging frankness that the play is artistically of small account, and that its author at the end of his life recognised the fact. In doing so, I think Mr. Ross has acted wisely. Honesty is the first essential in an editor, and nothing is to be gained by pretending that bad work is good—especially as in this case the pretence could take nobody in.

There will be some people, perhaps, who will urge that if a play is poor it is hardly worth exhuming after so many years, and that Wilde's reputation can only suffer by its publication. But this, I think, is a mistaken view. Writers of real distinction stand or fall by the best they produced, not by the worst. Byron and Wordsworth wrote plenty of inferior verse, which is duly entombed in the collected editions of their works. But no sane person pretends to think the less of their genius on that account. If *Vera* and *The Duchess of Padua* were far worse plays than they are—*Vera* could hardly be that, by the way—it would still be desirable that they should be published. Wilde is a writer of quite sufficient power and accomplishment to deserve the compliment of a complete edition. Moreover, the early work of great writers has an interest for intelligent people out of all proportion to its intrinsic merit. Ibsen's early plays are frankly bad for the most part, and no one can pretend that the actual artistic loss to the world would have been great if they had vanished as completely as the lost plays of Aeschylus. But they are interesting for the indications they contain of certain tendencies in his genius, and of the lines on which that genius was to develop, and for this reason the critic would regret their disappearance, though he cannot pretend that there is any particular aesthetic pleasure to be derived from their perusal.

From this point of view, it must be confessed, the early plays of Wilde are less illuminating, for there is far less of Wilde in the early Wilde plays than there is of Ibsen in the early Ibsens. *Lady Inger of Osträt* is a poor play with an elaborate intrigue constructed on absurd Scribe lines—and not very well constructed. For, whereas Scribe's construction is always clear and workmanlike, *Lady Inger's* is involved and tenebrous. Mysterious strangers pop in and out of dimly-lighted chambers, and nobody, either on the stage or in the auditorium, is allowed to know who they are or what they are about. When the Stage Society performed the play a season or two ago in London only a small fraction of the audience succeeded in disentangling the plot. This is quite remarkable in a play by the man who was to evolve the superb technique of the "social dramas." But though *Lady Inger* is a preposterous play, the eye of faith can see in it something of the Ibsen that was to come. There is an austerity and simplicity in the dialogue, an absence of mere rhetoric for its own sake, and a relative naturalness in the character drawing and the incidents which differentiate it from the work of his predecessors, and herald, faintly but surely, the rising of a new school of drama. Wilde's early work is less prophetic. There are moments in *Vera* and *The Duchess of Padua* when the dialogue or the characterisation gives a foretaste of the later comedies. The talk between the Russian Cabinet Councillors in *Vera* reads rather like a parody of the talk between the men in Lord Darlington's rooms in *Lady Windermere's Fan*, while Padua's Duke is a sort of blank-verse Lord Illingworth. And there is the same faculty for working up an exciting theatrical scene, the same fatal tendency to rely upon rhetoric instead of simplicity in emotional scenes, which made—and marred—the author's plays almost to the end. But except for this, the early drama gives no hint of the later work. The reason, of course, is simple enough. Wilde as a playwright was always an imitator rather than an original artist. In him, in fact, the faculty of imitation was carried to a point that was almost genius. He had an extraordinarily keen sense of literary style. If he had had ambitions in that direction he might have become a literary forger of the first distinction worthy to rank with Chatterton or Simonides. And, as was natural, this imitative faculty of his had the fullest play in his earliest work. Every artist begins by imitating some one. Even the greatest genius does not spring full-born from the head of Zeus. After a time he "finds himself," and ceases to be an echo, but in the beginning he models himself on others.

The difficulty about Wilde as a playwright was that he never quite got through the imitative phase. *The Importance of Being Earnest* is the nearest approach to absolute originality that he attained. In that play, for the first time, he seemed to be tearing himself away from tradition and to be evolving a dramatic form of his own. Unhappily it was the last play he was to write, and so the promise in it was never fulfilled. Had his career not been cut short at this moment, it is possible that this might have proved the starting-point of a whole series of "Trivial Comedies for Serious People," and that thenceforward Wilde would have definitely discarded the machine-made construction of the Scribe-Sardou theatre which had held him too long, and begun to use the drama as an artist should, for the expression of his own personality, not the manufacture of clever *pastiches*. It would then have become possible to take him seriously as a dramatist. For, paradoxical as it may sound in the case of so merry and light-hearted a play, *The Importance of Being Earnest* is artistically the most serious work that Wilde produced for the theatre. Not only is it by far the most brilliant of his plays considered as literature. It is also the most sincere. With all its absurdity, its psychology is truer, its criticism of life subtler and more profound than that of the other plays. And even in its technique it shows, in certain details, a breaking away from the conventional well-made play of the 'seventies and 'eighties in favour of the looser construction and more naturalistic methods of the newer school.

Consider its "curtains" for a moment and compare them with those of the conventional farce or comedy of their day or of Wilde's other plays. In the other plays Wilde clung tenaciously to the old-fashioned "strong" curtain, and I am bound to say he used it with great cleverness, though the cleverness seems to me deplorably wasted. The curtain of the third act of *Lady Windermere's Fan*, when Mrs. Erlynne suddenly emerges from Lord Darlington's inner room, and Lady Windermere, taking advantage of the confusion, glides from her hiding-place in the window and makes her escape unseen, is theatrically extremely effective. So is that of the third act of *An Ideal Husband*, when Mrs. Chieveley triumphantly carries off Lady Chiltern's letter under the very eyes of Lord Goring, who cannot forcibly stop her because his servant enters at that moment in answer to her ring. It is a purely theatrical device only worthy of a popular melodrama. But it produces the requisite thrill in the theatre. On the analogy of these plays one would expect to find in *The Importance of Being Earnest* the traditional "curtains" of well-made farce, each act ending in what used to be called a "tableau" of comic bewilderment or terror or indignation. Instead of this we have really no "curtains" at all. Acts I and II end in the casual, go-as-you-please fashion of the ultra-naturalistic school. They might be the work of Mr. Granville Barker. Of course, there is nothing really go-as-you-please about them save in form. They are as carefully thought out, as ingenious in the best sense, as the strong "curtain" could possibly be. But this will not appear to the superficial observer, who will probably believe that these acts "end anyhow." Here is the end of Act I:

Algernon. Oh, I'm a little anxious about poor Bunbury, that is all.

Jack. If you don't take care, your friend Bunbury will get you into a serious scrape some day.

Algernon. I love scrapes. They are the only things that are never serious.

Jack. Oh, that's nonsense, Algy. You never talk anything but nonsense.

Algernon. Nobody ever does.

(CURTAIN.)

This may seem an easy, slap-dash method of ending an act, and one which anybody can accomplish, but it is very far from being so easy as it looks. To make it effective in the theatre—and in *The Importance of Being Earnest* it is enormously effective—requires at least as much art as the more elaborate devices of the earlier comedies. Only in this case it is the art which conceals art which is required, not the art which obtrudes it.

In *The Importance of Being Earnest*, in fact, Wilde really invented a new type of play, and that type was the only quite original thing he contributed to the English stage. In form it is farce, but in spirit and in treatment it is comedy. Yet it is not farcical comedy. Farcical comedy is a perfectly well recognised class of drama and a fundamentally different one. There are only two other plays which I can think of which belong to the same type—*Arms and the Man* and *The Philanderer*. *Arms and the Man*, like *The Importance of Being Earnest*, is psychological farce, the farce of ideas. In it Mr. Shaw, like Wilde, has taken the traditional farcical form—the last acts of both plays are quite on traditional lines in their mechanism—and breathed into it a new spirit. Similarly, *The Philanderer* is psychological farce, though here there is less farce and more psychology. Unluckily, the Court performances of this play were marked by a dismal slowness and a portentous solemnity by which its freakish humour and irresponsibility were hidden away out of sight, and its true character completely obscured. Properly played, it would prove, I believe, one of the most amusing and delightful things in Mr. Shaw's theatre.

* * *

The same imitative quality which prevents one from taking *The Duchess of Padua* seriously as a work of art mars the comedies also. As far as plot and construction are concerned they are frankly modelled on the "well-made play" of their period. Indeed, they were already old-fashioned in technique when they were written. The long soliloquy which opens the third act of *Lady Windermere's Fan* with such appalling staginess, and sends a cold shiver down one's back at each successive revival, was almost equally out of date on the first night. Ibsen had already sent that kind of thing to the rightabout for all persons who aspired to serious consideration as dramatists. Luckily the fame of Wilde's comedies does not rest on his plots or his construction. It rests on his gifts of characterisation and of brilliant and effective dialogue. Both these gifts he possessed in a pre-eminent degree, but in both of them one has to recognise grave limitations. His minor characters are generally first-rate, but he never quite succeeded with his full-length figures. He is like an artist who can produce marvellously life-like studies or sketches, but fails when he attempts to elaborate a portrait. Windermere and Lady Windermere, Sir Robert and Lady Chiltern, none of them is really human, none of them quite alive. As for the principal people in *A Woman of No Importance,* Lord Illingworth himself, Mrs. Arbuthnot and her son, Hester Worsley, they are all dolls. The sawdust leaks out of them at every pore. That is the central weakness of the play, that and its preposterous plot. But when you turn to the minor characters, to Lady Hunstanton and Lady Caroline Pontefract and Sir John and the Archdeacon, how admirably they are drawn! Did anybody ever draw foolish or pompous or domineering old ladies better than Wilde? Think of Lady Hunstanton's deliciously idiotic reply to poor Miss Worsley when that American young lady, with impassioned fervour, has just been proclaiming to the assembled company the domestic virtues of her countrymen who are "trying to build up something that will last longer than brick or stone." "What is that, dear?" asks Lady Hunstanton with perfect simplicity. "Ah yes, an Iron Exhibition, is it not, at that place which has the curious name?" How it sets before us in a flash the whole character of the speaker, her gentleness, her stupidity, her admirable good breeding as contrasted with Miss Worsley's crude provincialism! Or again, think of that other reply of hers when Mrs. Allonby tells her that in the Hunstanton conservatories there is an orchid that is "as beautiful as the Seven Deadly Sins." "My dear, I hope there is nothing of the kind. I will certainly speak to the gardener."

* * *

When I say that it was only in his "minor characters" that Wilde was completely successful, I do not mean unimportant characters, or characters who only make brief appearances in his plays, such as the walking ladies and gentlemen in his evening parties, or the impassive men-servants who wait upon Lord Goring and Mr. Algernon Moncrieff. I include under the description all the people who are not emotionally of prime importance to the plot. Lady Bracknell and the Duchess of Berwick are very important parts in the plays in which they appear, and Wilde obviously took an immense amount of trouble with them, but they are not emotionally important as Lady Windermere is or Mrs. Erlynne. In that sense they are minor characters. It is in the drawing of such characters that Wilde is seen absolutely at his best. Who can ever forget Lady Bracknell's superb scene with Mr. Worthing in *The Importance of Being Earnest*, when she puts that gentleman through a series of questions as he is "not on her list of eligible bachelors, though she has the same list as the dear Duchess of Bolton"? Who can forget the inimitable speech in which she sums up the sorrows of the modern landowner?

"What between the duties expected of one during one's lifetime, and the duties exacted from one after one's death, land has ceased to be either a profit or a pleasure. It gives one position, and prevents one from keeping it up. That is all that can be said about land."

Yes, Lady Bracknell is an immortal creation. She is in some ways the greatest achievement of the Wilde theatre, the fine flower of his genius. It is impossible to read any of her scenes—indeed, it is impossible to read almost any scene whatever in *The Importance of Being Earnest*—without recognising that for brilliancy of wit this play may fairly be ranked with the very greatest of English comedies. But though Lady Bracknell is wonderfully drawn, she is not profoundly drawn. As a character in so very light a comedy, there is, of course, no reason why she should be. I merely mention the fact lest she should be claimed as an exception to the statement that Wilde's more elaborate portraits are all failures. Lady Bracknell is brilliantly done, but she is a brilliant surface only. She has no depth and no subtlety. Wilde has seen her with absolute clearness, but he has seen her, as it were, in two dimensions only, not in the round. That is the weak point of all Wilde's character drawing. It lacks solidity. No one can hit off people's external manifestations, their whims and mannerisms, their social insincerities, more vividly or more agreeably than he. But he never shows you their souls. And when it is necessary that he should do so, if you are really to understand and to sympathise with them, as it is in the case of Mrs. Arbuthnot, for example, or Lady Chiltern, he fails.

Why he failed I do not know. Possibly it was from mere indolence, because he was not sufficiently interested. Possibly he could not have succeeded if he had tried. To analyse character to the depths requires imaginative sympathy of a very special kind, and I am not sure whether Wilde possessed this, or at least possessed it in the requisite degree of intensity. He had a quick eye for the foibles of mankind and a rough working hypothesis as to their passions and weaknesses. Beyond that he does not seem to me to have gone, and I doubt whether it ever occurred to him to examine the springs of action of even his most important characters with any thoroughness. So long as what they did and the reasons assigned for their doing it would pass muster in the average English theatre with the average English audience, he was content. That is not the spirit in which the great characters of dramatic literature have been conceived.

The fact is, Wilde despised the theatre. He was a born dramatist in the sense that he was naturally equipped with certain very valuable gifts for writing for the stage. But he was not a dramatist from conviction in the sense that Ibsen was or that Mr. Shaw is. Ibsen wrote plays, not because play-writing seemed a particularly promising or remunerative calling in the Norway of his day. It did not. He wrote plays because the dramatic form irresistibly attracted him. Mr. Shaw writes plays because he believes in the stage as an influence, as the most powerful and the most far-reaching of pulpits. Wilde's attitude towards the theatre was utterly different from either of these. He wrote plays frankly for the market and because play-writing was lucrative. Of course, he put a certain amount of himself into them. No artist can help doing that. But no artist of Wilde's power and originality ever did it less. His plays were frankly manufactured to meet a demand and to earn money. There is, of course, no reason why an artist should not work for money. Indeed, all artists do so more or less. They have to live like their neighbours. Unhappily, Wilde wanted a great deal of money, and he wanted it quickly. He loved luxury, and luxury cannot be had for nothing. And if an artist wants a large income and wants it at once, he generally has to condescend a good deal to get it. Wilde condescended. He looked around him at the kind of stuff which other playwrights were making money by, examined it with contemptuous acumen, saw how it was done—and went and did likewise. The only one of his plays which seems to me to be written with conviction, because he had something to express and because the dramatic form seemed to him the right one in which to express it, is *Salome*—and *Salome* was not written for the theatre. When Wilde wrote it he had no idea of its ever being acted. But when Madame Bernhardt one day asked him in jest why he had never written her a play, he replied, equally in jest, "I have," and sent her *Salome*. She read it, and, as we know, would have produced it in London if the Censor of Plays had not intervened. But when Wilde wrote it, it was not with a view to its ever being performed, and so his genius had free scope. He was writing to please himself, not to please a manager, and the result is that *Salome* is his best play. *The Importance of Being Earnest* is written with conviction, in a sense. That is to say, it is the expression of the author's own temperament and his attitude towards life, not an insincere re-statement of conventional theatrical ideas. But *The Importance of Being Earnest* is only a joke, though an amazingly brilliant one, and Wilde seems to have looked upon it with the same amused contempt with which he looked on its predecessors. Perhaps he did not realise how good it was. At least he treated it with scant respect, for the original script was in four acts, and these were boiled down into three and the loose ends joined up in perfunctory fashion for purposes of representation. I wonder whether there is any copy of that four-act version still in existence, by the way? It is just possible that a copy is to be found at the Lord Chamberlain's office, for it may have been submitted for license in its original form. If so, I hope Mr. Ross will obtain permission to copy it with a view to its publication. If the deleted act is half as delightful as the three that survive, every playgoer will long to read it. But that a man of Wilde's theatrical skill and experience should have written a play which required this drastic "cutting"——or should have allowed it to be so cut if it did not require it——is an eloquent proof of his contempt for play-writing as an art.

Yes, Wilde despised the drama, and the drama avenged itself. With his gifts for dialogue and characterisation, his very remarkable "sense of the theatre," he might have been a great dramatist if he had been willing to take his art seriously. But he was not willing. The result was that in the age of Ibsen and of Hauptmann, of Strindberg and Brieux, he was content to construct like Sardou and think like Dumas *fils*. Had there been a National Theatre in this country in his day, or any theatre of dignity and influence to which a dramatist might look to produce plays for their artistic value, not solely for their value in the box office, Wilde might, I believe, have done really fine work for it. But there was not. And Wilde loved glitter and success. It would not have amused him to write "uncommercial" masterpieces to be produced for half a dozen *matinées* at a Boxers' Hall. His ambition —if he can be said to have had any "ambition" at all where the theatre was concerned—did not lie in that direction. So he took the stage as he found it, and wrote "pot-boilers." It is not the least of the crimes of the English theatre of the end of the nineteenth century that it could find nothing to do with a fine talent such as Wilde's save to degrade and waste it.

OSCAR WILDE AND THE THEATRE

James Agate

[1947]

According to Robert Ross, Oscar Wilde "never regarded his works as an adequate expression of his extraordinary genius and his magnificent intellectual endowment". And in *De Profundis* Wilde wrote:

> The gods had given me almost everything. I had genius, a distinguished name, high social position, brilliancy, intellectual daring; I made art a philosophy and philosophy an art; I altered the minds of men, and the colours of things. . . . Whatever I touched I made beautiful in a new mode of beauty. . . . I awoke the imagination of my century so that it created myth and legend around me. I summed up all systems in a phrase and all existence in an epigram.

Suppose we have a look at these extravagant claims. Genius? Wilde was a magnificent talker and a superb wit, and perhaps one mustn't complain that the wit all came from the same fount. A Jew, on being asked whether his dinner-table could accommodate twelve persons, answered, "Yes, God forbid!" And in the sense that all Jewish jokes are a form of this joke, so all Wilde's jokes are basically epicene. The "distinguished name" and "high social position"—neither of which Wilde possessed—were pegs for snobbery of the worst type; the photographs show him to have been insepar-

152

able from top hat and fur coat, with an unhappy lean-
ing towards astrakhan. Of the "intellectual daring" I
see no trace. He could rattle about the philosophy of
art in an amateurish way, but to say that he "altered
the minds of men" is just nonsense. As for "the new
mode of beauty," one might say that he could not
resist turning velvet into plush. "Myth and legend"?
Gilbert's Bunthorne is the answer.

Then that boast about being "a lord of language."
Wilde was that very different thing—the fine lady of
the purple passage. Apart from his wit, he was bogus.
The words "art" and "artist" appear on almost every
page of his writings; yet he knew very little about
the arts. In the matter of pictures Whistler was constantly putting him right. In the matter of music Wilde
could make one of his characters say, "And now, let
me play Chopin to you, or Dvorák? Shall I play you
a fantasy by Dvorák? He writes passionate, curiously
coloured things." No person with any knowledge of
music could have written this. About his own profession: "From the point of view of literature Mr
Kipling is a genius who drops his aspirates. From the
point of view of life, he is a reporter who knows
vulgarity better than anyone has ever known it. Dickens
knew its clothes and its comedy. Mr Kipling knows
its essence and its seriousness. He is our first authority
on the second-rate, and has seen marvellous things
through keyholes, and his backgrounds are real works
of art." The truth is that there is more knowledge of
life in six pages of Dickens or Kipling than in the
whole of Wilde's scented output. All the world known
to Oscar Wilde was what Pinero's Cayley Drummle
called "our little parish of St. James's." He was a
borrower, and his showpieces about jewels and such
like—how he would have hated the last two words!
—were lifted from the French. *Salomé?* The atmos-
phere was taken straight from Maeterlinck, and the
French from Ollendorff. Wilde was a fifth-rate poet
with one first-class ballad to his credit. His sonnet to
Irving ends with the astounding image:

Thou trumpet set for Shakespeare's lips to blow!

Wry-necked fife, yes, Trumpet, no. The plays? He wrote the wittiest light comedy in the language; the other pieces are stilted, wholly insincere society melodramas redeemed by their wit. If it were true that Wilde altered the mentality of his age, then that could have been written of him which was written of Swinburne: "He was to young men everywhere an intoxication and a passion, awakening half-formed desires, hidden longings and impulses, and secret enthusiasms, and wielding sway more imperiously over heart and sense and soul than any other man of his time did over the intellect or the reason of his disciples." Would one have written that of Wilde? Perhaps. But in the sense that young men to whom he was an intoxication were of the oddest kind.

Wilde's plays are, apart from their wit, the purest fudge, put together without any kind of artistic conscience, and using all the stalest devices of the theatre —concealed persons who give themselves away by upsetting a chair, brooches which turn into bracelets and thus throw a searchlight on the dark past of blackmailing ladies. Plays in which the situation is essentially false. A woman in humble circumstances has a baby. Twenty years later her betrayer, who has now become a powerful peer, offers the woman his name, coupled with a post for the boy as his private secretary— two offers at which any woman in her senses would have jumped. But not Mrs Arbuthnot. She explains to her son, now clerking in a bank, that she is a leper not to be purified by fire. An outcast whose anguish waters cannot quench. A lost soul to whom an anodyne cannot bring sleep nor poppies forgetfulness. To which, of course, the bank clerk ought to reply, "For heaven's sake, mother, come off it!" No, not all the wit in Mayfair can sweeten that little tract called *A Woman of No Importance*.

It may be amusing to see what contemporary critics thought about *An Ideal Husband*. Mr Shaw found a modern note in "Sir Robert Chiltern's assertion of the individuality and courage of his wrong-doing as against the mechanical idealism of his stupidly good wife." Archer, apparently holding that a notice of a witty play must also be witty, began by inventing a sub-title—*The Chiltern Thousands*. He found the piece "a very able and entertaining piece of work, charmingly written wherever Mr Wilde can find it in his heart to *sufflaminate* his wit." No body more impressive than our Archer when William's learned sock was on! May one suggest that the basic English for "sufflaminate" is to "put a sock in it"? Last of the London critics, the ungammonable Walkley wrote of "well-dressed men and women talking a strained, intense, but rather amusing idiom, while the action, the dramatic motive of the play, springs from the conventional devices of the commonest order of melodrama."

In the provinces Montague, after dismissing characters and action in terms of "the blackmailing lady who keeps whole catacombs of dark pasts" and "the brooch which becomes convertible against the nature of brooches, into a bracelet," called attention to the idleness of Wilde's thinking and invited the reader to compare "the cutting of the ethical knot here, when the wife and husband are relieved, not from his past act of profitable baseness, but from the mere fear of its detection, with the facing of the same difficulty by Ibsen in *A Doll's House*." One critic called the play a "heap of stale loans". Perhaps "fresh loans" would have been more accurate. Modern research suggests that Frank Harris offered Wilde the plot, and that Wilde jumped at the offer. I can well believe that this was so; I should have much greater difficulty in thinking that this wittiest of playwrights took the slightest interest in what emotions Lord X was feeling between paradoxes, or what Lady Y was meditating between *bêtises*.

I say that even in 1892 the serious half of *Lady Windermere's Fan* was stillborn. None of the women whom Wilde pretended to take seriously ever begin to come to life; his Lady Windermere is not only a puppet, but a puppet manifestly imbecile. Imbecile, too, in Wilde's own day and time. That her imbecility was not remarked was due to the fact that the public of Wilde's day was too much dazzled by Mrs Erlynne to examine closely into Lady Windermere. Mrs Erlynne, being a witty creation, is much better drawn. She is also very nearly the first example on the modern English stage of the courtesan, or something of that sort, being treated sympathetically. Paula Tanqueray did not burst upon London until the following year. It is true that Marguerite Gautier made periodic and cometary visits to these shores; but we are to remember what the famous cartoon of Du Maurier proves, that the audiences of those days went to the theatre determined to ignore that lady's character and to enjoy the actress's fireworks. Up to the date of Wilde's play paramours and the like were, God bless everybody, things of nought, and playgoers were so staggered and bedazzled at being asked in the new play to take one erring and another would-be erring woman seriously that it did not occur to them to examine whether the women were probable or not. Mrs Erlynne is redeemed by her wit, for if a character is witty enough nobody cares whether it is true to life or not. Whereas Lady Windermere is the complete goose.

Last remains *The Importance of Being Earnest,* a masterpiece and probably the best light comedy in the language. To attempt to say anything about this to-day is like opining that gold glitters and that silver shines. Let us see what was thought in 1895. I quote from that dour Scot, William Archer, who could never be said to laugh easily. "What can a poor critic do with a play which raises no principle, whether of art or morals, creates its own canons and conventions, and is nothing but an absolutely wilful expression of an irrepressibly witty personality? Mr Pater has an essay on the tendency of all art to verge towards, and merge in, the absolute art—music. He might have found an example in this play, which imitates nothing, represents nothing, means nothing, is nothing, except a sort of *rondo capriccioso,* in which the artist's fingers run with crisp irresponsibility up and down the keyboard of life. Why attempt to analyse and class such a play? Its theme, in other hands, would have made a capital farce; but 'farce' is far too gross and commonplace a word to apply to such an iridescent filament of fantasy. Incidents of the same nature as Algy Moncrieff's 'Bunburying' and John Worthing's invention and subsequent suppression of his scapegrace brother Ernest have done duty in many a French vaudeville and English adaptation; but Mr Wilde's humour transmutes them into something entirely new and individual. Amid so much that is negative, however, criticism may find one positive remark to make. Behind all Mr Wilde's whim and even perversity, there lurks a very genuine science, or perhaps I should rather say instinct, of the theatre. In all his plays, and certainly not least in this one, the story is excellently told and illustrated with abundance of scenic detail. Monsieur Sarcey himself (if Mr Wilde will forgive my saying so) would 'chortle in his joy' over John Worthing's entrance in deep mourning (even down to his cane) to announce the death of his brother Ernest, when we know that Ernest in the flesh—a false but undeniable Ernest—is at that moment in the house making love to Cecily. The audience does not instantly awaken to the meaning of his inky suit, but even as he marches solemnly down the stage, and before a word is spoken, you can feel the idea kindling from row to row, until a 'sudden glory' of laughter fills the theatre. It is only the born playwright who can imagine and work up to such an effect." Well, that's handsome enough.

On a day in November 1940, I found something German in my mail. Opening it distastefully I read: "Es scheint meine zu sein. Ja, da ist der Riss, den sie durch den Sturz eines Gower-Street Omnibus in jüngeren und glücklicheren Tagen davon trug. Hier ist der Fleck am Futter, der durch Explosion eines

alkohol-freien Getränkes in Leamington entstand. . . ."
And so on. Gower Street omnibus? . . . Leamington?

These struck a chord. I turned to my bookshelf and
I read. "The bag seems to be mine. Yes, here is the
injury it received through the upsetting of a Gower
Street omnibus in younger and happier days. Here is
the stain on the lining caused by the explosion of a
temperance beverage, an accident that occurred at
Leamington." It was Tschenberg's translation of *The
Importance of Being Earnest,* with the title *Ernst Sein!*
Moncrieff has become Montford, Lady Bracknell is
called Lady Brancaster, the gardener Moulton is given
a line, and there is a new character, Mr Gribsby, of
the firm of Gribsby and Parker, Solicitors. The play
is in four acts, the second being divided into two to
make room for the additional scene of Algernon's
threatened arrest for debt. The fun in the act that
Wilde deleted is better than any living playwright can
do. Algernon is being arrested for debt, and the bailiff
says: "Time presses. We must present ourselves at
Holloway Prison before four o'clock; after that hour
it is difficult to obtain admission. The rules are strict
on that point."

Wilde's fame is sure. Sure, in regard to this masterpiece, as long as audiences enjoy wit. Sure, in the
matter of the other three plays, as long as actors and
actresses like dressing up, and stage producers like
functioning as dressers.

SELECTED BIBLIOGRAPHY

Auden, W. H., "A Playboy of the Western World: St. Oscar, the Homintern Martyr," *Partisan Review*, XVII (April, 1950), 390-394.

Bentley, Eric, *The Playwright as Thinker*, New York, 1946.

Ellmann, Richard, "Romantic Pantomime in Oscar Wilde," *Partisan Review*, XXX (Fall, 1963), 342-355.

Foster, Richard, "Wilde as Parodist: A Second Look at *The Importance of Being Earnest*," *College English*, October, 1956, pp. 18-23.

Ganz, Arthur, "The Meaning of *The Importance of Being Earnest*," *Modern Drama*, VI (May, 1963), 42-52.

Gielgud, John, "Introduction" to *The Importance of Being Earnest*, London, 1949.

Kronenberger, Louis, *The Thread of Laughter*, New York, 1952.

McCarthy, Mary, *Theatre Chronicles 1937-1962*, New York, 1963.

Pearson, Hesketh, *Oscar Wilde: His Life and Wit*, New York, 1946.

Reinert, Otto, "Satiric Strategy in *The Importance of Being Earnest*," *College English*, October, 1956, pp. 14-18.

Roditi, E., *Oscar Wilde*, Norfolk (Conn.), 1947.

Toliver, Harold E., "Wilde and the Importance of 'Sincere and Studied Triviality,'" *Modern Drama*, V (February, 1963), 389-399.

Wilde, Oscar, *The Importance of Being Earnest: A Trivial Comedy for Serious People in Four Acts as Originally Written*, New York, 1956.

————*The Letters*, edited by Vyvyan Holland, New York, 1962.

————*The Original Four-Act Version of The Importance of Being Earnest*, edited by Vyvyan Holland, London, 1957.

Winwar, Frances, *Oscar Wilde and the Yellow Nineties*, New York, 1940.

Woodcock, George, *The Paradox of Oscar Wilde*, New York, 1949.

RECORDINGS:

With John Gielgud and Edith Evans: Angel Records 3504-B (2 records).

With Maurice Evans and Leueen MacGrath: Theatre Masterworks, Volume III (2 records).